HORNCASTLE'S

Hero or Hell Raiser

HORNCASTLE'S
Hero or Hell Raiser

Charlie Jacobsen: an ancestor of the Horncastle family

Graeme Horncastle

Natalya all the best.
(2019)

PAVILIONS

Published by the Pavilions Hotel Ltd
42 Papanui Rd, Christchurch 8144, New Zealand
Phone: 03-355-5633
www.pavilionshotel.co.nz

First published 2015

ISBN 978-0-473-31786-7

Production: Bradstock Editorial Services, Raumati South
Designed by Mark Winstanley / Go Ahead Graphics
Printed in New Zealand

Contents

DEDICATION

I dedicate this book to my late Aunty Phyl (Phyllis Ivamy, daughter of Charlie) for all the help and support over the years of writing. And to his living children for their stories: Jean Rutherford, Eric Jacobsen, Myrtle Freeth and David Jacobsen.
Also to Bruce Ivamy (grandson) for tying together years of research. And to Jane Baird (*née* Jacobsen) for her dedication to the wider generations of the Jacobsen family.

ACKNOWLEDGEMENTS

As with my previous book, *Horncastle's Suitcase*, I have to thank my wife Maureen as my spelling is so bad I can only write when she is at home.
To my brother Les and my sister Mary Smith who have helped out so much over the last five years.
Also to acknowledge that Phyllis Ivamy and Eric Jacobsen (children of Old Charlie and Mary Jacobsen) passed away while the book was being written.
Thanks to Mike Bradstock as he formed the book between us; and to Mark Winstanley who designed the book and presents it in the form you see it.

Graeme Horncastle

Preface

Why make such a big thing about a man called Jacobsen in a story about the Horncastle family? Simple really. First it's because he's our other grandfather and as such he represents half of the heredity that makes the Horncastles what they are today. Second, because he lived such an interesting life that his story should be better known.

Charlie Jacobsen begat my mother, who with my father Jim Horncastle begat those of us who survive today and represent the fifth generation of Horncastles. We were all born over a long time period so we span both the Baby Boomer generation and Generation X. Many people of this generation did well out of the opportunities that post-war redevelopment provided, but as you saw in my first book *Horncastle's Suitcase* and will see again in these pages, the Horncastles and Jacobsens didn't particularly benefit from all that. We did it by sheer hard work and drive and the love of a family.

It's ironic but my father James Horncastle was the most privileged member of the first few generations in my family and yet he had the least skill and initiative to hand on to us. There are hints of it here and there: he was a highly intelligent man who appreciated the value of education. He was no slouch and had a practical bent. He was a very skilled boatbulder, and he had the gift of the gab. His father (my other grandfather Henry, whom you will meet in my next book *Horncastle's Tales)* was a successful company manager though he too had his ups and downs. But when it came to exploring my family history it was Charlie Jacobsen who stood out from all the rest. He had lived such an interesting life that he blitzed the rest of the field: champion sportsman, winner of one of the first Royal Humane Society medals in New Zealand after trying to save someone from drowning; war hero, gold miner, launch master, prominent citizen in the remote Marlborough Sounds community – and the first in New Zealand to find uranium, which is an amazing story even if it didn't actually make him rich.

Right from when he was a little kid he was getting up to adventures that kids these days can't start to imagine, and he never gave up on that desire to discover new horizons even as an old man. Charlie Jacobsen, known to generations of Sounds and French Pass people as "Old Charlie" to distinguish him from his son "Young Charlie", led such an interesting life getting in and out of scrapes that you couldn't fail to notice him.

Grandparents are an important part of the family unit, but our grandchildren (like us before them) look on "old" people not thinking of the lives we have led, because their young minds only live in the now. As grandparents, my wife Maureen and I also make sure that we too live in the now as much as we can. Our children (their parents) need help and support and we try our best to do what we can, but of course sometimes they think we are meddling too much and can be told with a sharp tongue or held at a distance. I suppose we need it.

The *Noeline* after one of its numerous mishaps. Slipways are for maintenance, but for Charlie they were also for repairs after running aground or hitting rocks.

But back in the 1950s and 60s things were different. There were sayings like "Children should be seen and not heard." Thinking about it today, it was a terrible thing to say, as was the beating of children. We have come a long way from all that. But my old grandfather – my mother's father, Charles Jacobsen – was from the old school, and he was always a bit distant when he came to stay at our farm in Karamea (a 12-hour drive from his home at Picton). He had very little time for us and we only saw him as a wizened little old man with white hair and fingers missing on each hand. Of course, after he'd had a drink or two he would tell us stories of how he lost them. Whether he'd lost them in the war, to a saw, or to fish hooks, he told the story differently so many times he probably was no longer sure himself how he'd lost them. We watched in amazement as he rolled his cigarettes as fast as anyone who had all their fingers.

It wasn't until years later we wanted to know his story and my mother unraveled bits and pieces as we became old enough to understand the war and the way of life all those years ago. He died in 1960 when I was only eight, so I got most of the story secondhand anyway. Then my own mother died when she was just 47 so her recollections of his life became lost to me forever.

When I was in my thirties my Aunty Phyl gave me 30 pages of notes he had written down describing the early part of his life. Years later, at 58 I rang her to ask if she would mind if I wrote his life story. Aunty Phyl and I were good mates and she was ill and didn't have many years to go. She agreed that I should write it and said she had another 30 pages that had never been looked at. What a find!

I started working on Charlie's story while I was writing my first book, *Horncastle's Suitcase*, about my parents' and my own life. This book has been very popular. Now, more than fifty years after his death my grandfather's story is still worth telling so here goes.

Introduction

Charlie could change from a rugged-looking regular Kiwi bloke into a tidy-looking gentleman just by putting on a suit.

People often say to me, "How do you start a story like this?" and yes, that is the hard part. In a way you have to forget how you want to write the story and put yourself in the mind of the reader to hold their attention throughout. I decided to start with a typical story about my grandfather to help you, the reader, understand the character of the man in his fading years. The following story shows the hell raiser side of this man and will give you a taste of what's to come.

One morning in the quiet seaside town of Picton the old men and shift workers were enjoying a quiet drink in Oxley's Hotel when "Old Charlie" Jacobsen swaggered in the door, ranting and raving after a two-day binge, talking about the war, boats, gold or mineral prospecting. He was an expert on everything though his womanising days were fading with the years. His launch the *Noeline* was berthed only a hundred yards away at the town wharf. He was supposed to be in town for stores, household goods and spare parts for the launch, but didn't do much of the shopping himself. Mainly he did his ordering from the sanctuary of the pub and got one of his cronies to pick everything up and load it on board. Old Charlie was not your usual kind of alcoholic but still was a hell raiser whenever he hit town. Everybody in the pub had had enough of him and one of the young men told him so: "We're sick of listening to all your shit, why don't you just piss off?"

Charlie sized him up but backed down because even in his drunken state he knew he was losing more fights than he won as age was taking its toll on him. So he finished his drink, left the pub and staggered across the road. It was time to go home while the going was good. He fired up the old Gardner motor, which blew black smoke as he threw off the mooring ropes and steered out of the harbour. The men in the Oxley watched from the large bay windows, muttering about "good riddance" and wondering how long it would be before he would show his face again.

Then suddenly they saw the launch swing away from the main channel and head straight towards the shore. One of the fishermen said, "The silly old bugger has turned too early!" Half a dozen of them jumped in a car and drove around the waterfront in time to see the *Noeline* run hard up the sandy beach with Charlie sound asleep, arms draped over the steering wheel, the launch still in gear and full ahead but going nowhere.

They jumped on board, killed the revs and put the motor out of gear. A couple of them grabbed Charlie and took him down below, still out to it, and threw him on his bunk to sleep it off. Luckily the tide was rising and soon they were able to push the launch off the sandy beach. On this occasion there was no damage – unlike some of his previous drunken mishaps. They drove the launch back to the wharf, tied her up and went back to their own quiet drinking, no doubt having a good story to tell to anyone who'd listen that day.

Next morning the boat was gone. Old Charlie must have woken up and stolen away during the night.

This was my grandfather all over. He knew a lot of stuff about a lot of things, though he had very little education. He could get into trouble and out again like an octopus from a jar. One minute he was a top-notch seafarer and the next he was on the rocks. He was a shocking drinker, womaniser and bully whenever he could get away with it. He was a risk-taker and had more lives than a cat. His stories are often stranger than truth, though sometimes it's hard to know what's true and what isn't.

So where did this all begin? Let's start by going back to his ancestors.

CHAPTER 1

Charlie's ancestors and their early days in New Zealand

Charlie's grandfather, Johann Siegmund Martin (Isaac) Jacobsen.

Charlie Jacobsen, my maternal grandfather, was a second-generation New Zealander. His grandfather was an immigrant shipwright, Johann Siegmund Martin (known as Isaac) Jacobsen. According to family legend, as a reward for some great deed by Isaac's father, a police fire inspector of Norwegian ancestry, the boy was rewarded with an excellent education. Isaac received training in architecture and engineering with the Hamburg harbour board and at age 19, in December 1842 he embarked for New Zealand on the German immigrant ship *St Pauli,* arriving in Nelson on 14 June 1843. The 1849 Census records his address as Bridge St, Nelson.

The New Zealand Company's agent in Hamburg had widely promoted the benefits of settling in this new land and arranged the charter, which took the second wave of immigrants who arrived just a few months after the first ship the *Fifeshire*. The *New Zealand Journal* reported that about a hundred immigrants were on this second ship and that they were expected to make a great contribution to the development of the colony: "No emigrants are more valuable than the Germans, and we hail the announcement of the intended cultivation of the vine by them with unfeigned pleasure."

This was early in the days of the company that had been set up by a bad egg called Edward Gibbon Wakefield to colonise the Nelson region – a venture that was doomed from the start. Wakefield's promises of abundant, fertile land proved to be false and there was little work to be found, so the settlers suffered great hardships. The *St Pauli* arrived just a few days before a tragic massacre of settlers known today as the "Wairau Affray" that resulted from disagreements with the local Maoris over land ownership.

Soon after arriving, Isaac married Clara Franks, whom he had met during the voyage. These people were my great-great-grandparents, which makes me a fourth generation New Zealander. The first of their eight children, Anna Maria, known as Mary, was born in 1844. By that time half of the Germans who had immigrated to the Nelson province had already given up and left, many for South Australia. A few others formed their own communities at Sarau (today known as Moutere) and Neudorf. One time when there was a serious food shortage in Nelson, Isaac sailed an open boat across to Wellington to obtain supplies and made himself very popular with the desperate settlers on his return. Even the flour sacks were used to make clothes.

Although many settlers left disappointed, Isaac and Clara obviously made a good fist of it in their new home. He found plenty of work and built many fine early buildings, including the original Nelson Boys' College on Waimea Rd. He was

Auckland Point in Port Nelson, long before the area was reclaimed.

always putting up tenders to the Nelson Provincial Council to construct works like the Motueka wharf, warehouses, wharf offices, courthouse, lock-up and fencing the Queens Gardens, bridge over the Maitai River, extensions to the lunatic asylum and re-flooring the Collingwood bridge. Their second and third daughters Julia and Clara were born in 1847 and 1849.

Soon he sent for the rest of his family too, but it wasn't until April 1850 that his parents Hans and Anna sailed from Gravesend, England, on the ship *Mariner*, 683 tons, arriving in Nelson on 20 September that year. With them were Isaac's three brothers, my great-great-great uncles Johann Christian Jacob (known as Jacob), Johann Andreas (Andrew), and Johann Julius Heinrich (Henry). All of these men were carpenters. Now the whole family was reunited in Nelson and they all became naturalised New Zealanders within six months of arrival.

In the meantime he and Clara had a growing family, with their fourth child and first son, Peter, born in 1851, followed by Joseph (Charlie's father and my great-grandfather) on 8 December 1852. They all continued the family tradition of working in carpentry, building, architecture and shipbuilding.

Isaac was a man of many skills and was hardworking and enterprising. He built a vessel called the *Maria Josephine*,

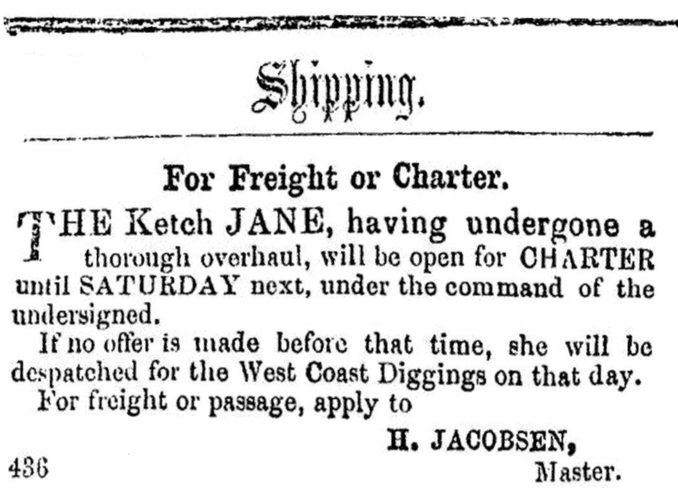

Shipping.

For Freight or Charter.

THE Ketch JANE, having undergone a thorough overhaul, will be open for CHARTER until SATURDAY next, under the command of the undersigned.

If no offer is made before that time, she will be despatched for the West Coast Diggings on that day.

For freight or passage, apply to

H. JACOBSEN,
Master.

436

An 1862 advertisement for the services of the ketch *Jane*, which played a significant role in the early settlement of the west coast.

which regularly traded between Nelson and Lyttelton, and lived for a while in Christchurch where he is said to have built many fine buildings and was credited with designing the first drainage system to convert the great Otautahi swamp into dry land on which to build the new city. But he found the damp climate did not suit his health and soon moved north again.

Charlie recorded that my great-grandfather Joseph and my great-great-uncle Peter built a house in Bridge Street when they were 12 and 14 years old and that it was still in good order 90 years later. I expect they were doing their apprenticeships at the time and their father and possibly uncles as well were keeping a pretty close eye on things.

In April 1860 Henry Jacobsen completed and launched at Nelson a small ketch of 20 tons and named it after his wife Jane (*née* Flowers), whom he had wed in 1857. A contemporary newspaper report said, "As this little vessel will only draw two feet of water at the stern, she will be highly serviceable for crossing bar harbours, and for river carriage." Henry skippered the vessel, which at first traded between Nelson, New Plymouth and Onehunga. With the prevailing westerly wind on this coast, they were usually sailing along a lee shore. This would have required great skill and seamanship because the west coast of the North Island and the port of Onehunga were very treacherous and claimed many vessels both large and small.

Soon the *Jane* was to earn a place in history by taking the first European settlers to the west coast. This region had been little explored by Europeans since the explorers Brunner and Heaphy had arrived there after several epic attempts to follow the Buller River all the way down to the sea. Heaphy was not upbeat about prospects for settling the coastal plains but in 1858 another explorer, John Rochford, took another look. He spoke more optimistically of the fine harbour and healthy climate of the Buller River mouth. Perhaps he saw it in fine calm weather when the river was low and the sandflies had taken a day off. By 1860 the government agent James Mackay had negotiated a large land purchase along the west coast for £300 and the first gold-diggers were trying their luck at Westport, though they did not stay for long.

In June 1861 a party of 14 chartered the *Jane* to take them from Collingwood to the Buller River area and bring in supplies to open a trading store and prospect for gold. Among other historical events, the British flag was raised at Westport for the first time during this trip.

It is hard to imagine this 23 metre ketch working her way up and down the west coast of the South Island. My brother Les works a fishing boat out of Greymouth and he can only work about a hundred days a year. The rest of the time the weather is too bad to take even his modern, high-powered 18 metre launch to sea. This makes me just think of our great-great grandfather leaving the safety of Golden Bay with no weather forecast and heading into the wild waters of the west coast. From here on he had a lee shore and only river mouth ports with surf and treacherous sandbanks and no navigation aids. If the weather suddenly turned against him there was nowhere to go except stay in the open sea or perhaps sail a couple of hundred miles past Greymouth to Jacksons Bay. There was no possibility of signaling for help or receiving any assistance if things went wrong. He was all on his own.

Think of this small ship tacking against the wind, waves breaking over her half the time. Living conditions on board atrocious with every area inside the boat wet and a bucket on deck for a toilet. Even the toughest of the passengers

The Grey River bar, from the north side about 1865.

throwing up day after day with seasickness. With the smell of vomit, sewage and unwashed human bodies in close quarters, you really had to want to find that gold or that patch of land to start your dream.

I visualise Henry sitting in his small cockpit, steering alone in the middle of the night with waves breaking all around him and often coming over the bow or foaming over the windward side of the vessel. Calling down for the crew every so often to adjust the sails. These tough men secured to the boat with lengths of rope in case they got washed overboard.

Even after all that, the most dangerous part was still to come, arriving at the river mouth. Working the tide to get enough water to cross the river bar, then going up the snag-infested rivers to unload and pick up freight, with no cranes in those day for lifting. It was just plain hard work and danger all the way. Henry was never shipwrecked himself, but later did lose his father on the Westport bar.

Henry told his story to the historian Carl Pfaff:

> These, with the men I took in the ketch, were the first permanent settlers and gold diggers on the west coast. We found about half-a-dozen Maoris living in Westport. There was no accommodation of any kind, so we had to set to work to provide some. The Maoris gave up one of their whares

A bush whare.

> [huts] for us to put the stores in. The country was a mass of dense bush everywhere. Mosquitoes, fleas, sandflies and blowflies were very plentiful. The blowflies were a perfect pest, getting into clothing, blankets and wherever they could. I waited for three weeks in Westport assisting the diggers (who afterwards scattered up the Buller River) with their stores. [A month later, Andreas Jacobsen tendered successfully to the Nelson Provincial Council to build the first navigation beacons at the mouth of the Buller River.] I continued to trade between Nelson and Westport for about six months; on one trip, I took among other cargo, three hundredweight [about 150 kg] of greenstone.
>
> I then went to Waimangaroa where I myself tried gold digging. Failing to get any gold there, I went further up the Buller, but met with no luck. Returning to Westport, I had the misfortune to lose my boat, and all it contained, coming down the river. I managed to swim ashore, a distance of nearly a mile owing to the difficulty of landing, and then did the rest of the journey on foot.

This was the adventurous beginning of both European settlement and successful gold mining on the west coast. At the time, though, it was completely overshadowed by the much bigger gold rushes in Otago and Marlborough. As Philip Ross May wrote in *The West Coast Gold Rushes*, "The *Jane* had arrived in Nelson with 120 ounces of Buller gold; the escort had arrived in Dunedin with 21,090 ounces of Tuapeka gold. It was an unequal contest." Much of the early gold was found at a locality in the Buller Gorge known

Buller River, Westport. Photograph taken by Frank Arnold Coxhead between about 1864 and 1890.

We believe this to be the *Jane* at Charleston. Although it appears calm in this picture, this spot is usually very exposed to the prevailing westerlies. If you've ever been there you will appreciate what a dangerous place this was for shipping, especially under sail power alone.

as the Old Diggings, close to where Charlie Jacobsen would find uranium 94 years later (see Chapter 14). Even later in the 1860s Westport did not quickly become a boomtown like Greymouth and Hokitika.

The year 1861 ended tragically when the family patriarch Hans died, aged 63, in a boating accident on 24 December while attempting to land at Westport from a small boat off the *Jane*. He was on his way to visit son Henry, who was still prospecting for gold at the time. Reported in *The Colonist* two weeks later, the accident took place when Hans and three other men were rowing ashore in calm conditions with the mail. As they crossed the bar a wave came up suddenly and swamped them,

> throwing the men into the sea to struggle for their lives ... the four men clinging to her as well as they could with the sea breaking over them continually. After being in this perilous situation for nearly half-an-hour a whaleboat, whose crew had been outside fishing, picked up the three men, Mr. Jacobsen having held on with the assistance of others until almost the last moment, but becoming exhausted with the struggle a breaker carried him away just before help reached them.

The body was not found until two weeks later, on the beach at Mokihinui. The men who found him had no choice but to bury him above high tide mark and pile a heap of stones up as a cairn to mark the spot. And so ended the story of one of New Zealand's significant early pioneers.

Today, whenever I pass through the area I like to stop by the sea there, pause and reflect on my ancestor's unmarked grave somewhere close by. This is all about reflecting on the amazing lives our forebears lived and not taking for granted the hardships they endured. I also think about my grandchildren – his great-great-great-grandchildren – and smile as I wonder what he would think if he could see them today, and what he would made of the modern world we now live in. History is fascinating and your own family history the most fascinating of all.

Henry had further adventures as the *Jane* continued trading to the west coast, but it was several more years before the great gold discoveries at Hokitika started a real gold rush. In March 1862 the *Jane* was chartered by the early Grey Valley settler Samuel Mackley to take him with his family and supplies to the Grey River. Also with the party was J. C. Richmond, an artist, editor of the *Nelson Examiner* and later a premier of New Zealand. While waiting to get into the Grey they sailed 50 miles further south so that Richmond was able to paint Mt Cook. After landing they travelled up the Grey River to Waipuna while the mate of the *Jane* took the vessel north to Westport again. Returning to the river mouth Henry noted that

Sketch map showing Henry's journey in 1862.

Buller River, Westport, sometime around 1865.

"...the Maoris were flooded out, the flat land where Greymouth now stands being six or seven feet under water. In order to reach the terrace at the back where we were to make our camp, we had to take the boat through the treetops." They then walked inland again and Henry had more harrowing experiences as he returned to Westport by canoe down the Inangahua and Buller Rivers, arriving after two days, in rags and tatters and half-starved. There to his shock he found the *Jane* up on the beach: "It had during my absence been sold with all it contained, by the mate who had also done away with the proceeds." Somehow he managed to get the vessel back and after that mostly traded in the Nelson and Golden Bay area until he finally sold it.

In September 1864 Henry took charge of a new sheep station, just the third established on the west coast, belonging to R. K. Newcombe and A. Domett, situated above the Grey River near the Ahaura. In January 1865 his wife Jane joined him there.

> Some idea of the difficulty of travelling at that time may be gathered from the fact that it took Mrs Jacobsen eight days to do the journey of twenty-five miles in a canoe owing to floods, rain, and other inconveniences. Canoes were the chief means of conveyance from place to place, but one journey from the station to the Grey had to be made in a raft (mokihinui) made of three bundles of flax sticks.
>
> The house in which my wife and I lived was built of mud, the walls being covered with moss halfway up. The roof consisted of flakes of manuka bark tied down with flax.

> The place was infested with rats of a very large size. The comforts or discomforts of living may be easily imagined. I left the sheep station after having been there nine months. ... Soon after this things began to improve very rapidly. Gold diggings broke out in several places on the coast and inland. Large sailing vessels and several steamboats were plying chiefly from Nelson and Melbourne, bringing people and stores of all kinds. Settlers and diggers were flocking everywhere.

The passenger steamer *Arahura* crossing the Westport bar. This picture is from a later era when sail had almost totally given way to steam and travel by sea had become much safer. Regular dredging meant the bar was safer and there were few shipwrecks there during the early twentieth century, though numbers did increase again after the fishing industry expanded in the 1960s.

Henry started gold digging again, this time on the Nine Mile Beach between Greymouth and Westport, but never made his fortune from gold. He became harbourmaster and signalman at the Westport bar from 1866 to 1875, with "hardly any rest, ten and twelve steamboats a day". Then he was transferred

Photograph of the Waterman's Arms, Westport, taken around the 1870s by an unknown photographer. A group of men are sitting and standing outside the hotel with the proprietor, G T Craddock, nearest the door and his daughter Maria standing in the doorway. A caged bird is hanging on the wall outside. In the doorway of the cottage next to the hotel are William Phillips and Mrs Pollock.

How the coastline at the Buller River mouth has changed over the years. In less than 150 years the coastline has radically changed so that the location where Hans was drowned is now dry land.

to Nelson where he operated the signal station for some years. In 1890 he was transferred to the Auckland district and became a signalman for the port of Manukau Harbour, a job he did not like. He wrote numerous letters complaining about his reduced salary and was evidently very bitter about being compulsorily retired about 1902.

Meanwhile, when my great-grandfather Joseph grew up, he moved to Puramahoi, on the western side of Golden Bay, to become a farmer. It was here that he met his wife-to-be, my great-grandmother. Mary Agnes Hailes was born in England in about 1859 and came out with her father, sister and brother in 1862 when her father took up a farm in Upper Takaka. Since 1856 gold had been worked in the area, and this provided the farmers with some useful income as they could sell eggs and butter for cash to the hungry gold diggers. More families came out from England and settled nearby, and soon the closest neighbour lived just eight miles away, so it became less lonely. They hacked a rough road out of the bush by cutting the trees down and pulling the logs to one side, without leveling off the ground. They had bullock wagons that went about as fast as you could walk, but because bullocks can pull a sledge in mud up to their stomachs they managed to get through in any weather.

Charlie recalled, "My father had quite a long way to go to do their courting. There were no roads and he had to go by boat first, then on horseback the rest of the way." Mary Agnes Hailes and Joseph Jacobsen were married on 25 October 1882. Mary produced three sons within three years, starting with Edward in 1884 and Walter in 1885. My grandfather Charles was next, on 1 August 1886. All were born at home at Puramahoi, and were among the second generation of New Zealand-born Jacobsens.

Charlie recalled what his mother told him the place was like in those early times:

> There were no roads, only tracks through the bush wide enough to get a horse and cart down, but muddy, without gravel. Mary's family owned two horses and I think her father had quite a bit of money to start off with. My mother was quite a good horsewoman, you had to be or walk everywhere. Her brother was 12 years old when he arrived so he was quite a help to his father: he had to work as hard as any man does today. My mother told me she had no boots to wear until she was about sixteen, and no school to go to but her father and sister gave her lessons. By the time she was seven she had to do all the cooking and washing as her sister and brother had to help her father clear the land for farming. Often they had no flour, sugar, tea or coffee, but they always had plenty of milk, potatoes and vegetables. There was only one store in Takaka and that was 18 miles away by bush track. All their stores had to be brought in by packhorse and on the way they had to cross the river five or six times. Everything had to come from Nelson on little schooners and occasionally Nelson ran out of stores so they had to live on what they grew on the farm, and could always get plenty of wild pigeon and kaka. They had their own pigs and very soon had their own sheep and cows.

The family was completed with the birth of Mary (junior) in 1888 and Alexander in 1890. Charles and his three brothers and one sister were all born over a period of just six years.

CHAPTER 2

Charlie's boyhood and the Royal Humane Society medal

Golden Bay was developing rapidly around the time Charlie Jacobsen was born in 1886. A second generation of settlers was established. Sawmilling was well established and the company of H. & T. Baigent was founded there in 1873, and Baigent Brothers in 1887. Takaka already had a post and telegraph office (opened in 1880), and within a few years it had a newspaper (1889) and dairy factory (1895). There was coal, limestone and iron ore mining as well as the gold that had been first discovered in 1856.

Charlie's mother, Mary Agnes *neé* Hailes.

My grandfather started school at five years of age but never had much time for book learning. He was far more interested in sport. The Jacobsens lived just 300 yards from Takaka Public School in Lower Takaka and Charlie was always early to get there in the mornings, especially in football season so he could have a game before the bell rang for class. They didn't call it rugby in those days: it was football, or footie. He was very keen on football and was getting pretty good at it when his brother Edward, who was two years older, had quite a bad accident during a game. He ran to catch a very high ball and misjudged the distance. The ball hit him on the side of the head and really knocked him about. Edward had a stiff neck for two or three years. Nowadays it'd be straight off the field and to the doctor after an accident like that but obviously nobody took the injury seriously at the time, he just kept on playing. I think he may have damaged something permanently.

Charlie's family: a photo taken after his father Joseph had died at age 52. Standing, from left: Charlie, Edward Jacobsen (who died at 24 years). Seated, from left: Mary O'Reilly (*née* Jacobsen), Mary Agnes Jacobsen (*née* Hailes), Walter George Jacobsen. Sitting on floor: Alexander Robbie Jacobsen (who died at 33).

Their father was concerned about the effects of this injury and decided not to let Charlie play in any matches. He was very disappointed but there was nothing he could do about it. Kids didn't dare disobey their fathers in those days unless they were prepared to risk a real hiding. If Charlie *had* disobeyed him and played any more games, in a small community like that his father would have found out pretty quickly anyway. He recalled sadly in his diary, "it wasn't until after I left school and went to live in Collingwood that I was able to play quite a lot of football." Some things never change across the generations – all kids think their parents are too protective sometimes.

Charlie had been a very keen swimmer since his earliest days and this became his main sport.

> I used to go to the swimming pool when I was four with the rest of the big boys. They used to think it was great fun to throw me in. I could dive across under the water before I

> could swim on the surface so I think that it is how I started to long dive. The pool would be at least 30 yards across and I could do that without very much effort. I will never forget the first time I swam on the surface. I was diving across under water and gave a big shove off the bottom, came to the top and did the same stroke that I was doing underneath. That's the way I learned to do breast stroke without ever being taught how. By ten years of age I could swim like a fish, in fact I spent more time under the water when it was clear, than on top. We all learnt to swim early at our school. It was a part of the school training and our master was very good himself.
>
> Now the first thing we learned about swimming was that you had to be able to swim a half a mile comfortably before you got any speed. It is something like roller-skating; when you get your balance you can do anything on skates. Swimming, you just swim. After a while you will find yourself on top of the water and you don't know how you got there. But you had to train hard, with skipping, club swimming, deep breathing, swimming a mile at moderate speed, taking long walks and going to bed early.

Another activity was hunting. In those days there were a lot more native birds around and nobody thought anything of shooting them. The word "conservation" hadn't been invented, and people needed to catch what food they could. It was open season on wild ducks, pigeon and kaka, which were all good to eat, and every boy learned to use a shotgun – the old-fashioned hammer gun, not the modern type with cartridges – as soon as he was strong enough to lift one and heavy enough to cope with the recoil. They had to learn how to reload in the field after each shot, using dry powder and caps. Keeping everything dry was all-important (remember that saying "keep your power dry"?)

Those old double-barreled hammer guns were pretty dangerous and they had some near-accidents with them. Nobody drilled into them the lessons about firearm safety that are routine nowadays – like never carry a loaded firearm when crossing a fence. Once when Charlie was getting through a wire fence the two hammers caught on the wire and both barrels went off at once, just missing him and Edward. After that he learned common sense and always put the gun through the fence first just to make sure of no accidents.

Golden Bay is well known for big floods and Charlie saw his share of them. When the Takaka River used to flood sometimes half the valley in Lower Takaka was under water, with the river six metres above normal and flowing at up to 25 km an hour. When there was a flood on they used to swim across the river to get to the best hunting spot, pushing the gun along in front on a piece of timber and carrying the powder and caps in watertight bottles. Edward and Walter, being the older brothers, used to do the shooting and Charlie was their retriever, who had to swim out and get the ducks.

To most people the idea of going swimming in a flooded river would be ridiculous but Charlie and his mates were very confident, and were among the first generation of New Zealanders who grew up unafraid of the water. Many of their forebears could not swim at all. Drowning was sometimes referred to as "the great New Zealand death" because crossing rivers was by far the commonest cause of fatal accidents in the early days. The explorer Charles Douglas famously said that not being able to swim had saved his life many times. Anyway, when there was a big flood Charlie and his mates used to walk about 5 km up the river and take off for the other side, swimming across as they were swept down. Soon they got to be able to read the water and knew exactly where they would end up on the other side, but sometimes they would almost be there when the swirling waters would suddenly sweep them back to the side on which they had started.

Although they were fit and confident in the water, they still had some very close shaves and Charlie was involved in more than one rescue.

The first incident took place when it was a hot day and he, his brother Alexander and the local schoolmaster's son, a boy named Lance, decided to go swimming in a millpond. This was large deep pond behind a wooden dam about three metres high with a floodgate controlled by a winch. When the gate was wound up water flowed fast along a water race to a big water wheel that drove one of the local flax mills. The millrace was about two metres wide and a metre deep.

They all dived in alongside the hand winch, forgetting that the floodgate was open. The suction of the water pulled John under. Charlie was a few metres away but Alexander saw him disappear and took a dive after him, then realised when he got near the opening what had happened. Charlie recalled later:

> I turned round and saw both of them had gone but did not know what had happened until Alex came up and said, "Charlie, you're the best diver, go and get Lance, I think he is stuck under the dam." I took a dive and found him jammed by one of the stringers but could not get back for the force of water, so I scratched my way under the stringer and dragged him after me. Worse luck we were only kids and did not know that there were three more stringers to scratch my way out, but luck was with me, the water flattened out a good bit and by turning over on my back I could get a part of my face out enough to breathe. So I turned Lance over, pushed his face up again at the bottom of the floor until I had scratched enough to pull him through the next one. The last one, dropped straight into 10 feet of water made by overflow when there was a flood on.
>
> By that time Alex thought we were both drowned and he was just going to get some help, not that it would have been any use, when I yelled out and he saw where we were. He plunged in and we got Lance ashore, turned him over on his face, got a flat board and rocked him up and down on it like a seesaw. After about 20 minutes Lance started to mumble. My brother then lit a fire and we gave him a big rub-down, slapped him all over and soon he was able to stand up. We took him home and my mother gave him some hot coffee and he didn't seem any the worse for his experiences, in fact I think I suffered the most because my fingernails were very nearly torn off. We never told Lance's father because we were scared he would give him a walloping. In fact later he found out anyway, and was always good to me for saving his son.

The floods in Takaka always carried a lot of driftwood and Joseph Jacobsen found a way to put this to good use. Firewood was always in demand so he built a platform on a willow tree that overhung the river and his boys used it as a base to snare logs drifting past. They learned to throw grappling hooks over floating logs, then check the rope around part of the tree and ease the log into the bank. If it was too big to lift out they would tie it up with wire until the floodwaters receded, then they would saw it into pieces they could handle. Soon they got quite expert at the job and enjoyed being 12-year-old "firewood merchants". Imagine parents allowing their kids to do this kind of thing today!

Then tragedy struck in February 1899 when a young boy called Ted Moulder came along and wanted to have a go. Charlie was chopping up some firewood for his mother at the time, when all of a sudden the rope caught around Ted's feet and pulled him into the water. Charlie's brother Alexander yelled out, "Ted's in the river!"

Charlie didn't hesitate, he just dived straight in, grabbed hold of Ted and tried to drag him ashore. Unfortunately the swirling waters dragged both of them out and away from the bank. Then they struck an eddy and were pulled under. Charlie managed to get Ted up to the surface again and told him if he felt the water pull them down again, to take a good breath. Unfortunately Ted could not swim and had no real idea how to hold his breath, so after they went under for the second time and came up again Charlie could see that Ted had taken a good deal of water and was gasping for breath. He realised he had no chance of getting him ashore as the bank was steep and the water was swirling outwards all the time, but there was an overhanging willow branch and he grabbed that with one hand while holding on to Ted with the other.

In the meantime Alexander had run to fetch their mother and she had called out to some men on the road but by this time the two boys were 30 metres from the bank and the men had no chance of reaching them without a boat. Charlie held on to Ted until eventually his coat pulled off and he was swept away (though Charlie thought Ted had already drowned before he let go).

Now it was a matter of rescuing the rescuer. Somehow Charlie managed to climb up and onto a fork in the tree, by which time he was so exhausted he had to lie down for half an hour. The men threw him a line and after a number of tries they managed to get it to him. But still Charlie was not out of danger. He tied the rope around and under his armpits and they began to haul him ashore but as they started to pull he became tangled in the willow roots and got jammed. No sooner had he got clear and managed to get to the surface when down he went again, right into the middle of a submerged blackberry bush. By this time he was completely exhausted and did not remember any more. Apparently the men just kept on pulling and he never came up to the surface again until he reached the shore, helped by another rescuer called James Haldane.

By this time everyone thought Charlie had drowned except their neighbor, Mrs Bodmore, who sprang to the rescue. She told his mother to fetch hot water and blankets, and they nearly rubbed all the skin off him, put him in hot water and blankets with mustard on them, and kept at him for hours until he came around. At one stage he reckoned he could see them all and hear them talking but could not move, and remembers that lady polishing a looking glass and putting it over his face – the old test for whether someone is breathing or not. Charlie said to himself, "Breathe or bust" – and he did breathe.

That's why he pulled through and we all have Mrs Bodmore to thank or none of his descendants would be here today. They kept Charlie in bed for three days and he soon got over it though Alex lost all his hair through shock. He was sure Charlie had drowned.

Newspapers throughout the country reported this incident and Charlie was made into a hero. There was an interesting aftermath to this event as it coincided with the establishment of the Royal Humane Society awards for bravery and a request for nominations "of any cases of saving life and of bravery displayed in doing so". The locals of Takaka found two deserving recipients and nominated them, and at a Nelson City Council meeting on 17 March their names were put forward: "Mr A. T. Maginnity [referred] to the bravery of two lads in the Golden Bay district – Samuel Westrupp, under 14 years, and [Charles] Jacobsen, aged 12. He suggested they should be presented

TWO RESCUES, TWO MEDALS – 63 YEARS APART

By an extraordinary coincidence, both my grandfather and I were awarded Royal Humane Society medals for attempting to rescue people from drowning. In my case I was a bit more successful because somehow I managed to save both the victims – which was just as well as they were my little brother Tom and my sister Mary.

It happened on the family farm at Karamea, when I was 11. They were floating in the river in a tin bath we played in as a boat, and right when they were in the middle of a deep pool, the bung popped out and the *HMS Tin Bath* quickly sank in water that was way over their heads. I dived in without thinking, while Christine ran for help. Fortunately we all came out of the incident unscathed, though Mary was unconscious and had to be revived – it was an incredibly close shave and all three of us might have died that day. You can read the whole story in *Horncastle's Suitcase*, concluding with my remark that I always thought it was pretty good getting a medal when it was actually myself who had allowed the little kids to get into the bath in the first place!

Two drowning rescues, two generations apart in the same family: my grandfather's Royal Humane Society medal and mine.
You can see these today in a display case at the Pavilions Hotel.

ROYAL HUMANE SOCIETY CITATION

Charles Jacobsen – *Certificate of Merit*

Charles Jacobsen, 12, schoolboy, of Takaka, Nelson, at personal risk gallantly attempted to rescue Edward Moulder, 8, from drowning in the Takaka River, on 6 February 1899. Moulder was snaring wood during a flood in the river, and having secured a log as it was passing, the rope he was using got caught round his leg and he was swept off into the strong current. Jacobsen immediately jumped into the water, and after a vain but gallant attempt to save Moulder, his own life was, with difficulty, saved by means of a rope from the shore.

with watches, and that the Royal Humane Society should be communicated with."

The other boy, Samuel Westrupp, had helped rescue a woman and her young children at Ferntown during the floods. In Nelson, there were two other nominations of boys who had saved a child from drowning in the Brook; but apparently Charlie's act was deemed more heroic.

As a result, the following year he was presented with the Australian Royal Humane Society Certificate and Bronze Medal, one of the first five awarded in NZ.

The people of the district also gave him a silver watch but he told the mayor that they should have given it to Mrs Bodmore because it was she who had saved his life.

Charlie also recalled a story about an early boating experience while he was just a baby, when the family nearly came to grief. They were paddling from Puramahoi to Takaka in a canoe when it sprang a leak – perhaps the plug came out, or something like that. Anyway his father had to paddle furiously while his mother laid him down in the bottom of the canoe so she could bail for her life. With cold water suddenly, unexpectedly sloshing all over him, Charlie reckons he must have howled his head off.

His father had a flat-bottom boat three metres long with a centreboard, two sails and a pair of oars. No lifejackets or safety equipment, of course. When Charlie was about 11 he and Edward took the boat from their home up the river down to the sea, quite a journey of about 10 km before they even got out into open water. Everything went well at first. They put the sail up and went out a few kilometres to get some snapper. They put down the anchor and caught a few fish, then decided to go home before the tide got too strong in the river. There was a good fresh sea breeze coming in, but the boys got a little careless and instead of holding on to the main sheet so they could easily release it in a hurry, they tied it off. Just as they came into the river the wind freshened and changed direction, suddenly they gybed and the boat turned over about 400 metres off the beach.

At first they were more concerned about losing their fish than anything else. They tried to swim while pushing the boat towards the shore but the tide was against them so they knew they had to right the boat and get into it again. Edward told Charlie to dive down and undo the mainstay and pull the mast out, which he did. They managed to turn her the right way up but were then faced with the enormous task of bailing out all the water. Eventually they got home but they didn't dare to tell their father what had happened for fear that he might not let them use the boat again. However, these things have a way of getting out and it turned out that a man standing on a hill about 5 km away had seen the whole thing, though it wasn't until six months later that he told their father. By this time the boys had been in plenty of other scrapes and their father didn't make a big deal of the boat incident. He probably had bigger things to worry about like how he was going to pay the bills, or where their next meal was going to come from.

High-diving platform that Charlie would dive off.

Meanwhile Charlie was improving his swimming skills and becoming ever more interested in swimming underwater. He got his first experience at it while helping a local man make a repair on a ship's hull at Collingwood. This man, a Mr Bishop, was an extraordinary diver who could hold his breath long enough to actually do useful work under water. He dived down and had a look at the hole that needed mending, then came up and got a piece of plank of the right size. He put six four-inch [15-cm] nails into the plank with a bit of canvas tacked to it then dived down and nailed it on while Charlie held it for him.

This experience had a great influence on Charlie. Now he started to train properly for swimming long distances under water. He used breathing and relaxation exercises to develop his chest expansion and endurance, and after a while he could hold his breath for 2½ minutes and swim a hundred metres quite easily on one breath. He reckoned that being relaxed rather than big and strong was the key: "There were four boys at my school that could swim 75 yards [about 68 metres] under water and we were all under 12 years old."

Then there was high diving. Soon after Charlie was born, there was a world-wide craze for daredevilry and death-defying stunts. It was a bit like the modern craze for base jumping and wingsuits, except that people were not ready to do it themselves yet. They just wanted to watch. A stunt man could always draw a crowd by making spectacular jumps off high structures like bridges and ships' masts. The Fitzgerald Brothers Circus capitalised on this craze by bringing a British high-diver called "Professor" Charles Owen Peart on their New Zealand tour in 1895. To promote the circus he used to do a high-dive off the top yardarm of a sailing vessel in the harbour. Charlie got to go and see the actual circus and decided to try and copy Peart's dive from a height of 45 feet [13 metres] into five feet [1.6 metres] of water. He was barely ten years old so this wasn't just daring: it was foolhardy. But Charlie was bulletproof like all young people and nothing would hold him back. With three of his mates he rigged up some scaffolding on top of the high diving board at the Takaka pool, to a height of about 16 metres. At first he practised diving from there into about three metres of water, always trying to see how shallow he could get.

> One morning there were only three of us in the swimming baths, so I said to them, "I am going to have a try. If I hit the bottom, pull me out before I drown." The previous day we had whitewashed the bottom of the swimming baths and when I climbed to the top and had a look down. it looked like it was only a foot deep. I took a big breath and swallow-dived. I did not go within [half a metre] of the bottom I could see as I turned. I did that dive half a dozen times that morning and then did it about 12 times every day until it was just like diving into [6 metres] of water. I did that dive I suppose over a thousand times, and also taught another young chap to do it.

In the meantime, "Professor" Peart had been killed in 1896 after hitting the side of his diving tank in Sydney. If word of this reached Charlie it certainly did not put him off, but soon he had a very near escape himself:

> One day there was a sort of carnival on, and we had a game of water polo. I swam in four races and did a long swim under water, about 96 yards. Then they asked me to do a high dive. I didn't feel like doing it as I had already done so much swimming, but I climbed up the scaffolding and looked down into the water. There was a slight wind blowing and the scaffold was swaying, and I didn't feel like it so I said to

> myself, "I'll just climb back down again." But the next thing I knew I was on the bottom of the pool in a daze, I had fallen and been knocked out for a few seconds. The water was red and my face was hurting. I could not have actually dived into it, otherwise I would have hit my hands instead of my head. I swam to the other end of the pool, walked into my dressing cubicle, and started to take off my swimming suit, when the secretary of the swimming club walked in. He was the only one of about 300 people present who realised what had actually happened. He sent for a doctor, who put four stitches in my forehead, two in my nose and four more in my cheek. I don't think anyone else found out what had happened until the next day.
>
> That was all right at the time but about 10 days later my ear started to ache in the middle of the night. I jumped out of bed and went to the same doctor who had sewn me up before. He had a look inside my ear, but could not find anything wrong, so told me to come back in the morning when a specialist would be there. In the meantime he gave me three tablets, told me to take them, blow the candle out and hop into bed.
>
> I slept all right but next morning when I went to the other doctor he just looked at me and said, "When did you get this cut on the face?" Then he gave my chin a sharp push. The pain was so great I very nearly hit him and I jumped about 3 feet in the air. He said, "You have a broken jaw and it is festering." He gave me something to ease the pain and the next day he operated and took a small piece of bone out. After that it very soon got better.

Still this experience did not put him off, for as we will see later, he continued to do some spectacular high dives later in life. But he never dived into shallow water again. Perhaps even at the tender age of 12 he had already learned that maybe he wasn't quite bulletproof after all.

Like most boys in those days Charlie only attended school until he was 13. Summer school holidays were shorter in those days, with only a fortnight at Christmas, but schools also closed for six weeks in the hop-picking season. There were about ten hop gardens in the district and everybody turned out to help. The kids looked upon it as the time of their lives, out in the open, sunburned and always hungry from the smell of the hops, having a good holiday and an opportunity to earn a couple of pounds.

The Christmas holidays provided an opportunity for the ultimate kids' adventure – going camping without any grownups around to supervise. Three or four of the boys would take a tent, a couple of billies to cook in, a camp oven, pick, shovel, and axe, flour, sugar and tea, a small box and a gold dish. Off they would go away back into the bush and do a bit of fossicking. They soon learned quite a bit about digging for gold but never had any big finds, just "colour" or fine gold. They just about managed to live off the land, with so many different birds to shoot and even fruit and vegetables like fuchsia berries, supplejack and fern tips and the delicious fruit of "giggy" (kiekie). They supplemented this by making damper (unleavened bread cooked on hot stones or in the camp oven), and returned home and went back to school again as fit as greyhounds. Nowadays it would be regarded as criminal neglect to let kids go camping like this, and you'd have to take your kids to Disneyland or something to give them anything like such a big thrill.

In the 1890s there were quite a lot of Maoris living in Takaka, and Charlie's father was a good friend of many of

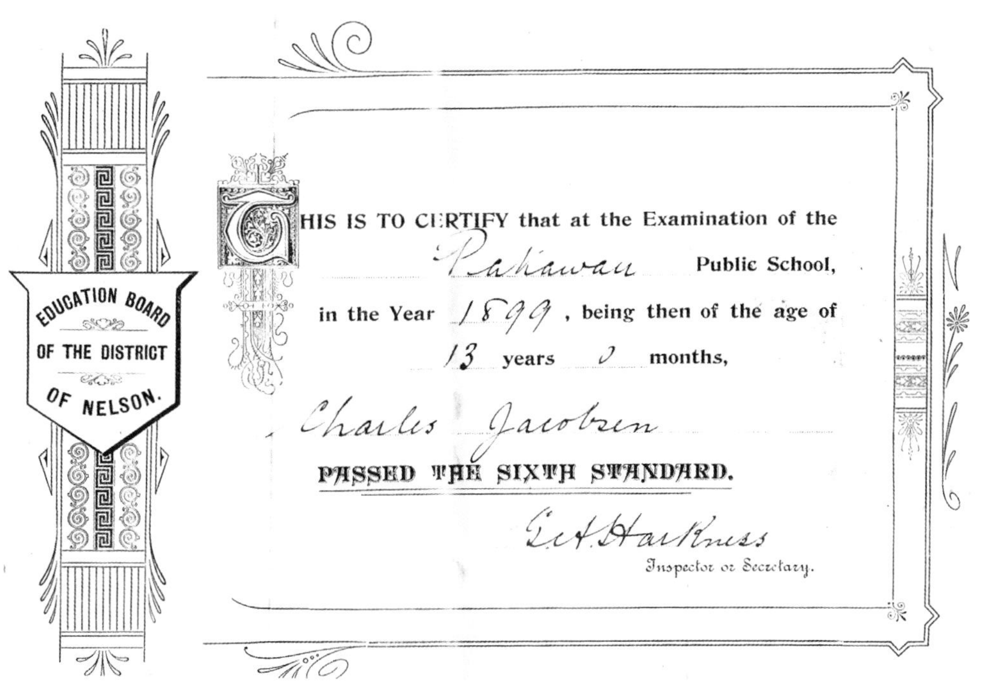
EDUCATION BOARD OF THE DISTRICT OF NELSON.

THIS IS TO CERTIFY that at the Examination of the Pakawau Public School, in the Year 1899, being then of the age of 13 years 0 months, Charles Jacobsen PASSED THE SIXTH STANDARD.

G. A. Harkness
Inspector or Secretary.

Charlie passed Standard Six or Form 2 and got a certificate to prove it, in 1899. This level is today known as Year 8, and was about as far as most children ever got with their education in those days.

them. He spoke Maori well and knew a lot of Maori songs. He was friendly with an old chief who had the full facial tattoo or moko. Charlie used to go with his father to visit him, but was scared of the old chap until one day he gave him an apple. It's amazing what small things can do and how a gesture like that can make all the difference, because after that he was never afraid of him again.

CHAPTER 3

Charlie's father Joseph and his mining ventures

There was not much opportunity for a good education in Charlie's time, especially living in such an isolated place, but the family had plenty of skills to pass down the generations. Charlie's father Joseph was a man of knowledge and entrepreneurship. By the time Charlie was a teenager his father had shown him the basics of mining and assaying and given him an instinct for investigating the opportunities of the new country's mineral wealth.

Charlie's father, Joseph Jacobsen, got him interested in mining at a young age.

A longing to find treasure seemed to run in the family, for Charlie was not yet born when his grandfather Hans claimed to have discovered diamonds in Canterbury. In 1883, Alford Forest in South Canterbury was the scene of a short-lived "diamond rush", when the word got out. Although local experts said his finds were not diamonds, he formed a public company that attracted a lot of interest, and sent samples to the UK for further testing. The reply came back that the stones were of "small value" although "a fair proportion of the stones were genuine diamonds". This only fuelled the excitement as optimists interpreted this to mean that bigger, more valuable stones must also be there. A number of other companies were formed. Speculation grew as further announcements were delayed (some said deliberately) and snow blanketed the area, making it difficult to prospect further to prove or disprove the claims. However, as the *Otago Witness* reported on 8 August, "plentiful as the diamonds are said to be, it is extremely difficult to get a sight of one," and while it was claimed that the diamonds could be obtained from the surface "by the cartload" it was clear that the reporter didn't believe a word of it ("If this is the case, why are such large amounts as £1000 and upwards required [to develop a mine]?")

The reporter was also rather scathing about Hans: "...the original discoverers or promoters ... cannot be altogether exonerated from the imputation of great carelessness and culpable ambiguity by countenancing the reports which are circulating, even allowing that they do not utilise them." This fell just short of an accusation that he was lying. Whatever the truth, the rush was soon over and nobody made any money from diamonds. To be fair, rumours of great mineral finds in Canterbury were frequent during the 1800s. All sorts of optimists continually struggled to find some mineral wealth in a region that was desperate to match up with the other provinces of the South Island. Finds of rubies, gold and other riches were also reported in Canterbury at various times, but turned out to be uneconomic finds or false alarms every time.

A similar question mark must also hang over Charlie's father Joseph's mining venture, the Hidden Treasure Company, which started operations in 1904 near the mouth of the Puramahoi Stream. Joseph's operation smelted ore from the Hidden Treasure Mine near the iron works at Onekaka. He died only a year later so his record of the venture is sketchy, and by the time Charlie got round to setting down his own version many years later, his memory was confused. This is not so surprising as there were some odd things about the whole venture from the start. It seems that Joseph reckoned he had discovered a new kind of metal that had never been found before anywhere in the world. That was impossible, because by that time all the elements, including all metals, had been discovered and identified.

It is more likely that the gold from the mine had other precious metals mixed in with it. This is nothing unusual. Newly mined, raw gold bullion often contains some silver and copper, and often also has other, very heavy metals including platinum and iridium – which are very valuable themselves and also make gold into a very hard alloy that is even more dense than pure gold.

Joseph Jacobsen called his metal alloy "chlor gold" and carried out a lot of experiments to separate and identify the metals in it all by himself. Charlie took much interest in the whole process and recalled watching as Joseph developed a way to mix his metal with purer gold to make a harder alloy that he said would be ideal for coinage: "This brilliant success will be a great boon to Great Britain, as for centuries experiments have been made by scientists to manufacture coins free from base metals, but without success..."

Not everyone believed this, but the mining venture got off with a hiss and a roar, with enough investors ready to put money up for a smelting works. On 12 March 1904 Mary Jacobsen laid the first corner stone of the works building and then "the visitors adjourned to a large tent, and were regaled by the Company with liquid and solid refreshment in great abundance." A man called Rowden Soper spoke enthusiastically of how prospects for the venture were no longer being looked at as "the product of the brain of a fool" and another speaker praised Joseph for his persistence "in spite of the greatest discouragements from all sides ... Cheers were then lustily given for the Hidden Treasure Company, for Mrs Jacobsen, Messrs Jacobsen senior [Hans] and junior [Joseph] ..." This is a sure indication that they had had to put up with some ridicule along the way, but for now Joseph's critics were silenced, presumably because of the early test results. He was manager of and part shareholder in a new mining venture.

A few months later, things were looking even better for the operation when *The Colonist* of 30 August 1904 reported that Joseph had just returned from having gold samples assayed in Auckland by an expert with the unlikely name of "Mr Bastard". The ore had supposedly yielded 50 ounces of gold to the tonne, which was fabulously rich (even just one ounce to the tonne was payable) and also contained platinum and copper. Joseph Jacobsen said with some pride that he had "been complimented on doing the work which scientists have been engaged upon for years."

But soon tragedy was to strike, with the death of Joseph

Jacobsen in a boating accident at Takaka on 2 October 1905 while crossing the bar in a sailing boat which overturned. The tragedy was widely reported and noted as a great loss in the district.

By 1907 the Hidden Treasure venture was all over, and the annual report of mines stated that the claims had lain idle since Joseph's death, though some of the ground "has been taken up for iron-deposits by Messrs. Jones and Wayne." This does not sound a likely outcome for a mining venture that was working rich deposits of precious metals and had a number of shareholders. Perhaps the ore was too patchy and ran out very quickly, or the investors may have been too optimistic about quick returns and gave up too soon. But that would still not explain why no one ever worked the mine again, and the mine is not even mentioned in passing in the histories of successful gold mining in New Zealand. The Hidden Treasure Mine became just another of the many mining failures that litter New Zealand's history.

There's also a big mystery about Joseph's precious metal. No specimen of it has survived and from the description it would have to have been platinum or iridium, and a lot of it. Look at what Charlie wrote about it in 1959:

> It was something like platinum to look at, very heavy. You could put it in a furnace for three days and nights and take it out it was the same weight as when you put it in. It could be rolled out thinner than a tissue of paper and had a ring like a piece of steel. I saw my father dissolve a piece in some acid, let it settle in a powder, then put it in a crucible and bring it back to the original metal.
>
> My father and I thought it might be lead. So we got a piece each of zinc, tin, silver and some of this stuff. Put them in separate crucibles and we took turns watching and stoking the furnace. The furnace was a coke and charcoal with a force draught. The lead disappeared in about 15 minutes, the zinc about the same. The silver lasted three to four hours, the tin about one hour. But this new metal of his was kept there for three days and nights and when we took it out it was just a few grains short of the weight that we put it in at. ... We used quite a lot of the metal for fishing sinkers when we could get a piece without my father knowing. They sent samples all

> over the world and got different assays from each place, but each place mentioned platinum. Some said a certain amount of osmium, some said iridium. It might have been a mixture of the whole lot, but they did not know how to separate them in those days ...

The use of the metal for sinkers is another puzzle. Surely their father would have kept track of every ounce of such a precious metal so that the boys could not have taken any more than a scrap of it without his noticing? Tests carried out by the expert assayers for identifying every element are quite straightforward and surely should have been able to determine exactly what the metal consisted of. So where does the truth lie? Did they briefly hit on a localised patch of precious metals that ran out as soon as they got into production? Just how much of it was there? Why has none of it ever been found again? Was someone "salting" the mine; and if so, whom?

Whatever the truth, the experience had a great effect on Charlie. It contributed to his lifelong interest in minerals and valuable metals, and was undoubtedly an influence upon his great adventure with uranium fifty years later.

I have discussed this story with mining and metallurgy experts and the conclusion we have reached is that the special metal is much more likely to have been tungsten. There was a fair bit of it being mined in the area and it fits Charlie's description in every detail. Tungsten never evaporates no matter how long you heat it in a furnace, and is one of the densest metals known. It is also not a precious metal, so that might explain how the boys were able to get some so easily.

Mining of iron ore in the area continued for many years but the gold was a duffer. Today there's a nudist colony near the spot and a walking track to the mine. It's also the spot where a new species of giant carnivorous snail called Gillies' land snail was discovered in 1930.

CHAPTER 4

Charlie's early working life

Charles Jacobsen was 13 years old when he left school in 1899 and went to work on a farm for 5 shillings a week. That's 50 cents in today's money but of course there's no comparison because five shillings in those days had the spending power of about fifty dollars now. So it wasn't good pay by today's standards but everything was different then, people didn't have material expectations like having more than one pair of shoes. There were also not many labour-saving devices, for example no milking machines, so it took three of them to milk just 45 cows.

On the first morning after they had done the milking, fed the pigs and calves and had breakfast, the farmer told Charlie one of his daily jobs was to shift a great big shorthorn bull that had a chain round his horns and a ring through his nose. The farmer kept this animal in a paddock by itself, chained to a large crowbar driven into the ground. When they went to open the gate to shift the bull it dug one of its horns in the ground, ripped up the ground up with its foot, stuck out its tongue, shook its head and roared. The farmer told him not to worry and that the animal was "as quiet as a sheep" so Charlie went up and stroked him on the forehead, then shifted the crowbar so that the beast could get some more feed. But he must have been very afraid because he told the farmer that was the first and last time he was prepared to do this job. He even reckoned he said, "That bull will kill somebody one day," and the farmer just laughed and said,

"You'll get used to him." But Charlie didn't get used to the bull, in fact the farmer never asked him to shift it ever again. Perhaps you will have already guessed what's coming: six months later when the farmer went on holiday he got his brother to look after the farm, and the bull attacked and killed him. So you see you can never trust a bull as far as you can throw one, which of course is not very far.

After that Charlie didn't stay much longer but went trucking in the Motupipi coal mines. The job was underground, dangerous and dirty, pushing and pulling wagons loaded full of coal, but it was great money at the time and Charlie felt like a little millionaire. However, the job only lasted about six months before the mine closed.

Then he got a job delivering meat and the mails to a group of miners working about 40 km away up the back of Collingwood. He would walk up there leading two loaded packhorses by the reins and ride one of them back after dropping off the goods. That must have been a very enjoyable part of the job, quietly wandering on horseback along the old gold trails in the valley.

He had several interesting experiences during this time. One was when a lady asked him to get her some Prince of Wales Feather ferns, a particularly beautiful kind of fern that was very common up the Aorere. She wanted some to grow in her garden. He picked some of these ferns and was just putting them in a bag with some moss to keep them fresh when suddenly he noticed what appeared to be a 20 cm long caterpillar with a fern growing out of its head. He looked around and noticed there were quite a number of them and was very surprised and puzzled by this discovery.

Someone later gave him a half-baked explanation but he never really found out the truth about these peculiar "plant/ animals". It was not until much later that he managed to get to the bottom of the mystery after meeting the Director of the Dominion Museum, Dr Oliver, following an incident where the ferry *Arahura* ran ashore in Billhook Bay in 1943.

What Charlie had found was in fact one of nature's great oddities, the so-called "vegetable caterpillar" or *Cordyceps*, a kind of parasitic fungus that invades the tissues of

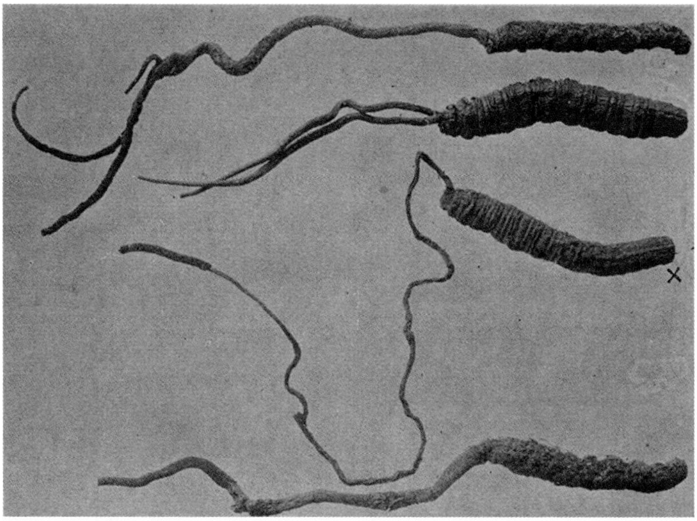

Vegetable caterpillars. From a 1920 paper by G.H Cunningham.

caterpillars in the ground. As it parasitises the caterpillar the fungus tissues grow and feed off it and turn the caterpillar into a lump of fungus with exactly the same shape. Then the fungus puts out a shoot that grows up and produces small branches that give off spores, completing the life cycle. It was this shoot and the branches that Charlie mistook for a fern. It's a pity that he was not able to find out more about this because vegetable caterpillars are highly valued for use in oriental medicines so he might have been able to make some money out of them.

Delivering the mail produced an unexpected dividend one day around 1904 when he made a delivery to an old man who lived in a hut by himself. Charlie had a cup of tea with

Fording point on the Slate River, not far from where Charlie had his narrow escape.

him while he read his mail. Suddenly the old man got very excited and announced that he had drawn the first prize in the big Australian lottery, Tattersall's (known as "Tatts"). Charlie had to take him back to Collingwood to claim his prize, and the old man gave him five pounds – equivalent to about three weeks' pay, a very generous tip indeed.

The mail always "had to go through" and Charlie took some risks crossing rivers at times and had at least one narrow escape from drowning while crossing the flooded Slate River on horseback shortly above where it joins the Aorere.

> The two packhorses were ahead of me and they crossed all right so I thought it was good enough for me. I got just about half way across, with the water up to my knees on the saddle, when my pony slipped. The flow took him off his feet so down we sailed towards the Aorere, but he swam out on the other side with me still in the saddle, both of us none the worse for taking a short cut home.

Another time he misunderstood the warning on a sign where the track crossed the tidal Pakawau River estuary, which was unbridged in those early days. The crossing was a 5 km trudge across a mudflat and a sign on the bank warned that the water was too deep for safe crossing when it was above a certain mark. Charlie didn't realise that this meant to say that he should wait until the water fell below that level while the tide was going *out*. The water level was below the safe mark but the tide was actually coming in, so he didn't have the time he thought to get across safely. "Had quite a swim that day," Charlie noted with typical understatement.

Every generation of children grows up with some war in the news and with Charlie it was the Second Boer War of 1899–1902. He was caught up in the excitement of it like most colonials in those days, when people were very patriotic. Charlie saw the Takaka Mounted Rifles being formed in 1900 with Captain J. J. Langridge in command. The corps numbered 64 men, each of whom provided his own mount and saddlery. He recalled with excitement the celebration that went on in May 1900 when the news came through about the relief of Mafeking, a town where the British troops had been under siege for seven months. This was the event that made the scouting movement founder Robert Baden-Powell famous, and was a great moment for the whole British Empire.

Some of the locals, Charlie included, decided to form the "Takaka Royal Artillery". The Takaka blacksmith and wheelwright, Mr Walker, who had previously been in the Nelson H Artillery Battery, knew how to make a small cannon out of steel pipe and sheet. At just this time my grandfather started an apprenticeship with Mr Walker and one of his first projects was helping him make a real cannon for them.

This photograph was taken at the Takaka Showgrounds at the celebrations to mark the end of the Boer War in 1902.
From left: Harold Emms, Charlie Jacobsen, Cliff Page, Walter Sanders, Harry Hitchcock, John Mason and Jack Madigan.

First they took a 5 cm pipe and welded a plug in the end, then they shrank another pipe over the top of that and built up more layers of steel the same way, finishing with a ring-shaped piece welded over the muzzle. The cannon was about a metre long, mounted on two wheels and drawn along by two horses, just like the six-pounder of the Nelson H Battery. They had a week's training and had to lead the celebratory procession.

Blacksmithing in those days was a good and brisk business to be in. In a remote place like Takaka the blacksmith had to be able to fix anything so there was nothing he couldn't fix. They had a lathe power stock and die, a power drilling machine, and a 20-hp steam engine and boiler, planing machine, and several other machines for the wheelwright business.

At this time Charles Jacobsen, a strapping young man in the prime of his physical strength, found another new passion: cycle racing. The newfangled bicycle had caught on all over the world, not just for getting around but as a sport. Cycle racing had been added to the Olympic games in 1896 and the first Tour de France was in 1903. The first race Charlie entered was a 14-mile (22 km) road race and he came second. That gave him the confidence to decide he would really stick at it for a while.

Charlie in his bike riding days.

He was a founding member of the Golden Bay Cycling Club in April 1904 when also he won the club's one-mile and five mile races. In the two-mile race he was just second: "Jacobsen spurted, and led the field for the last lap, but was passed in the straight."

The young man who beat him in his first race was a Bill Bates, the wheelwright Charlie worked with at Walker's. Bill came from Riwaka and was engaged to a young lady in Motueka. Most men worked Saturday mornings in those days and regularly at noon the two friends would set out to bike up over the Takaka Hill to Motueka where Bill would stay for the rest of the weekend. That's a big ride, 60 km over a hill 800 metres high, hard enough on a modern light racing bike, but these boys only had ancient bikes with no brakes or gears, and the roads were very basic. Then from Motueka, Charlie would press on another 50 km to Nelson to stay with his mother, arriving with enough energy to wander round the town with his mates until about ten, then go home to bed. He would rise punctually in the morning at six and go down to Trafalgar Park where there was a real luxury – an asphalt track he could ride on smoothly and just as fast as he could go. "I couldn't get my feet to travel fast enough," he said. He would set off from Nelson again about 1 pm on Sunday, meet up with his cobber Bill and both would be back in Takaka before dark. Literally they must have been as fit as champion athletes.

Their equipment really was very primitive. I mentioned earlier that they had no brakes on the bikes. For those long steep downhill runs on each side of the Takaka Hill they tried tying on a bunch of scrub from alongside the road and towing it behind. It worked best if the scrub was just heavy enough that they had to keep pedaling a bit. However, they soon got stopped from doing that because it made a noise that frightened horses. The first proper bike brakes they had were two rubber rolls that used to press down on the front tyre. They worked quite well if the road was dry, but if it rained the road got very muddy and with no mudguards they would soon get filthy from head to toe. They soon managed to get rim brakes for their back wheels.

Charlie completed his apprenticeship at age 19, in 1905. Since he now had his ticket, he was entitled to a tradesman's wage instead of the pittance paid to apprentices. But the boss reckoned the business couldn't afford to pay him more so he had to give Charlie the sack.

Charlie also got interested in ships for the first time about now. His friends the Stallard brothers, who worked at the Puponga coal mine, kept a yacht, the *Mapua*, 7 tons, at Waiotapu. It drew about six feet and was anchored near the wharf, where the water was always deep enough. When they wanted the vessel they used to ring up from Puponga and Charlie and one of his friends would take it round to them at high tide. The yacht had no engine but a good set of sails. With the dinghy they would tow her around the corner then raise the sails. Charlie would climb out on the gaff to make her heel enough to clear the bar, and then they would sail up to Puponga, pick up the Stallards and go places. Charlie enjoyed this enormously and said, "That's where I got my sea legs, and I also think that some of that salt water got into my bloodstream."

CHAPTER 5

A strange experience with nutmegs, and the Collingwood fire of 1904

Charlie and one of his mates were both picked to play football in the senior team but both were bothered by half a dozen boils on their arms. Someone told them to eat raw nutmegs as some kind of folk cure, but did not say how many to take at a time.

What the two lads did not realise was that nutmeg contains small quantities of two powerful hallucinogenic drugs, methoxysafrole and elemicin. There's nowhere near enough to affect you if you eat a curry with nutmeg in it, but it was a different story if you ate whole nutmegs:

> Well I ate seven and the other chap ate five, and it was the most peculiar experience that I had in my life. We happen to be in a billiards room, where two young chaps were acting the goat. We started to laugh and couldn't stop. That set all the others going so we decided to go home.
>
> I lived in a boarding house and he lived in a hotel owned by his mother. As soon as I got to bed it started to move up and down like a launch in a rough sea, so I grabbed the sides. Then it seemed to roll sideways, and I thought I could expand and float on top of the bed.
>
> All of a sudden I thought that I was going mad. There was a light in the corner right opposite my bedroom window, so I concentrated my thoughts on it and thought as long as I could remember that it was the hotel light, I would remain sane.
>
> Then I seemed to be able to hit out just as if I could knock the

> boarding house down. I would inhale and it seemed to me I could expand my foot.
>
> After a while I got very thirsty and tried to get out of bed but couldn't sit up. Another young chap had a bed in the same room. I tried to call out to him but I could only open my mouth, no sound came out, and there I lay until the girl came up to wake us in the morning. She saw me with my mouth wide open and ran downstairs for her life and told the boss. He came up and shook me like anything. I seemed to come out of a dream, got out of bed, went and had a shower, dressed and went for breakfast. But while drying my face I noticed that if I ran my finger across, it would leave a mark. Before going into the dining room I just put a circle on one side and a cross on the other, and they stayed there for over an hour.
>
> I went to work, lit the fire and was just starting to blow the bellows when I fell over. The boss took me outside, smelt my breath, and asked what I had been eating. When I told him nutmegs he asked how many. I said seven. He said, "It's a wonder you are alive. Go home and take three packets of Epsom salts and go to bed." I did as he said but couldn't sleep.
>
> The waitress came up, knocked at the door and came in to tell me that the other guy was off his rocker, that the doctor was with him and could not make out the trouble. I went to see him and the first thing he did was to try to haul off and hit me, but he had his hand clenched so tightly that his elbow wouldn't straighten out. Then I knew he had the same thing as I'd had all night. I told the doctor what we had been eating and he gave him something stronger than salts.
>
> The steamer was leaving Collingwood for Nelson the next day, 7 November 1904, and my boss told me to take a month off.

It had been an extraordinary 24 hours but fate had not finished pulling surprises on Charlie before he could leave town:

> I didn't sleep very well that night and at a quarter to one in the morning the fire alarm went off. A fire had started in Stallard's bakehouse as they fired up their ovens to bake bread for the next day. Somehow the chimney must have been faulty and the fire got into the ceiling of the bakery. I jumped

> out of bed and went to give a hand but by the time I got there the fire had taken hold. We tried to put it out but there was very little water available.
>
> By this time everybody realized that the whole town was in trouble. A strong westerly wind was blowing and the alarm became general so we all took to saving what we could out of the buildings. Children and women were hurried from their beds, taking what they could and wrapping themselves against the cold wind. By this time Stallard's boarding house was well and truly alight. Rait's store and dwelling were on fire as well and there was nothing stopping the fire. Soon it crossed the street to the Post Office and worked northward and southward very rapidly. The two hotels were fiercely burning at one time. The sight at 2 am was devastating and most of the town was burning. Kerosene cases and explosives were going up in the hardware store. Seven miles away the light was so bright in the sky it was possible to read a newspaper by it.
>
> My mate and I decided that we could do very little for the commercial part of the town and helped the people with their houses, getting their personal goods and belongings to safety. Rivals and enemies set aside all their differences and united in action for the general welfare of the town. Teeming rain had set in by 3 am and a dreary smoky morning broke over the town with tired, forlorn people keeping watch over their remaining belongings.
>
> People came from the country and other small towns with food and clothing and anything else they could carry which could be of help to the folks of the town. The telephone exchange was destroyed so they worked on that immediately to restore contact with the outside world. The total amount of the insurance claims was £10,000 but the losses amounted to £25,000.

The *Nelson Evening Mail* reported that "This morning the town is a blackened, smoking heap of refuse, surmounted by dozens of chimneys, not one solitary building being left fronting the main street." In all, 20 businesses were destroyed and Riley's store, on a side street, was the only one left standing. Halls, stores, a church, the library, the post office, billiard saloon, premises of the local newspaper, stables and a number of houses were burned to the ground. Timber stacked in sheds nearby went up.

Collingwood in 1898 ...

Although Charlie was still worn out from his terrible experience with dangerous drugs, he worked all day to help the folks of the town. He lost all his belongings in the fire, including his beloved racing bike. There was nowhere left to stay, so he took his passage on the steamer that night as arranged.

At a special service in St Cuthbert's Church the next Sunday, the Reverend Mr Quintell singled out Charles Jacobsen and a Mr McKeany for special thanks for their "heroic efforts". A newspaper report stated, "Strenuous

... and again just after the fire.

efforts on the part of Mr S.M. Riley and Messrs McKenna, junr, Jacobsen, Ahnfeldt, and others happily saved the former's residence, which was in imminent danger for some time."

I went home and my father took me to Dr Andrew. I explained what I went through with the nutmeg incident and the doctor wrote it all down. He said he had read about it but it was the first case he'd had anything to do with. He treated me for about three months and I gradually got over it. For months I could poke my finger in my arm or leg or face and it would leave an impression for quite a while. The other chap took more than six months before he was right.

My father bought me a new bike – he must have felt sorry for me. That was the only thing he had ever bought me in my life.

All the buildings in the main street were destroyed, and Charlie was among the many who lost all their possessions – including his precious racing bike.

The inquiry into the fire didn't pull any punches: "The sad loss shows the carelessness of Collingwood residents, as there seems to be no doubt that a small and regular supply of water would have put the fire out when it first originated." In December the Fire Relief Committee made a number of cash awards for "sufferers", including £5 to Charlie.

After Charlie got well he started with an engineering shop and worked there for quite a while. Apart from his work he was very prominent in cycling during this period, along with his younger brother Alexander. He was back in Collingwood in January 1905 to win the two-mile bike race at the New Years Day sports and regatta. At Richmond on New Year's Day 1906 he won both the two and five-mile races despite an 80-yard handicap in both events: "Jacobsen's win [in the two-mile race, i.e., 3.25 km] was a popular one, and he rode well and gamely. Time 5 minutes 11 3/5th seconds."

In 1907 he also played rugby as a senior for the Collingwood Football Club. He won the 3-mile [4.9 km] race at the Nelson Anniversary sports day in February in 7 minutes 37.4 seconds (in which Alex came third) but made a poor showing in the two-mile bike race at the Takaka Athletic and Cycling Club's winter sports day that year: "Ten started for this event but several dropped out before the finish. Jacobsen, the scratch man, made a very poor showing, far below any riding we have seen him do before." He didn't do much better in the five-mile race either. From about this time onwards Charlie tended to stick more to swimming and diving. Maybe he had decided that cycling was not his forté after all.

CHAPTER 6

The Golden Blocks mine

In 1906 Charlie got a job working as one of four chainmen on the first detailed geological survey of the west coast, with the director of the Geological Survey of New Zealand, Dr James Macintosh Bell. They started at Cape Farewell and worked their way south, exploring all the creeks and rivers from the sea to their source and the country around them. Bell was said to be very class-conscious and this may have meant that he regarded Charlie as a person of no great consequence. Perhaps that is why Charlie didn't leave a more detailed record of the experience, and didn't hesitate to throw in the job when a better opportunity came along.

One of Charlie's most lingering memories was that while working with Dr Bell they found "hacksaw blade fossils",

Photographed in 1908, the Canadian geologist James Macintosh Bell, his manservant and other members of his party pose outside the original Heaphy hut near the mouth of the Heaphy River. The hut was built as a base while geologists worked in the area.

Charlie was fascinated by graptolites, or "hacksaw blade fossils", found by the geologist James Macintosh Bell while Charlie was working with him as a chainman in 1906.

or graptolites, which looked like flattened plants with sawtooth-shaped branches but were in fact animals of a very ancient kind that are now all extinct. There were many kinds of them and they turned out to be very useful for matching rock types between one part of the country and another, and even with rocks in Australia. Fossils were interesting in their own right, but it no doubt increased Charlie's interest in geology to discover that the graptolites were from the same age of rocks (Ordovician, 490–440 million years ago) as those that contained gold.

There was already nearly a 50-year history of mining in the Golden Bay area (gold had been discovered in the 1850s) but gold mining in the bay had declined. However, two very profitable hard-rock mines, the Golden Ridge and the bigger and richer Golden Blocks mine were still in full operation. These were located in remote rugged hilly country between the Aorere and the west coast, called the Taitapu Estates, 25 km from Collingwood.

In 1907 while Bell's party were based nearby in a bush camp at Big River (just north of Kahurangi Point), a regular delivery of stores failed to arrive, so they sent Charlie up the coast and inland to the Golden Blocks Mine to collect the goods – a weight of about 32 kg. Charlie stayed the night with the storekeeper there, who mentioned that they needed a blacksmith so he went to see the mine manager, who offered him the job on the spot. The mine was expanding at the time with further exploration of new leads and prospects looked good for the future.

Golden Blocks (also called the Aorangi Mine) was possibly New Zealand's richest hard-rock goldmine at the time, averaging more than an ounce of gold per tonne. About 45 men worked there, many of them underground where there were thousands of metres of tunnels, galleries and shafts following the gold-rich quartz veins. Men on the surface operated stamper batteries that ground the hard rock into mud, then extracted the gold with mercury. The operation was so large that they had two blacksmith's workshops at different levels on the hills around the mine.

After Charlie had been there just a fortnight, the storekeeper left, so he took over the store and the post office.

He finished his smithing work at 4 o'clock in the afternoon and would then run the store and post office until 10 at night. He even became secretary of the local miners' union.

The process of gold extraction fascinated him:

> There was an eight-stamper and a four-stamper battery. The quartz carrying the gold was crushed with stampers weighing about half a ton, lifted up with cams then dropped about 1 ft 6 inches [45 cm]. The quartz was forced into a steel box containing the stamper and blocks which they banged down on. The quartz would be crushed between the two blocks until it was like flour and would pass through very fine gauze, and water was fed in at the same time. Then it was washed over copper plates. The copper plates had first been cleaned with cyanide of potassium, one of the most deadly poisons known, then mercury would stick to the plates and then the fine gold dust washing over would stick to the mercury.

The broken, hilly country of northwest Nelson was home to one of New Zealand's richest gold mines, the Golden Blocks, where Charlie worked in 1907–08.

> When we cleaned the mercury and gold mixture, which was called amalgam, it was put in chamois leather bags and as we would squeeze off as much of the mercury as we could. Then the rest was put in a retort. That consisted of a small cylinder with an outlet pipe screwed on. This pipe was put in a long tub of water; the cylinder with the amalgam was put into a furnace; the mercury evaporated, went through the pipe and condensed back into mercury again. This just left the gold in the retort. It was then put in a crucible with boracic acid powder and smelted into solid blocks. We had a kerosene furnace and it took a while to melt the gold.

About six months before Charlie started at the mine, the previous manager had taken some of the mine's gold and tried to sell 90 ounces of it to a bank in Wellington. The bank manager got suspicious and called the police, who arrested him. He owned up and handed over the rest of the gold, but got eight months' jail. In the meantime they put on another manager who Charlie had known for years, and who was quick to put his trust in him. This gave Charlie an interesting experience of resisting temptation, for he soon found himself in a position where he could have stolen a lot of gold himself.

It happened when the stamper box needed to be repaired and Charlie had to work all day Sunday so that the battery could start again as normal on Monday morning. The boss had warned Charlie there might be a little bit of gold amalgam caught behind the worn-out lining plate that he had to replace. "Just keep it in your hut," he said. "There won't be much. I'll get it from you when I come back from Collingwood on Friday."

> It was a major job cutting the half-inch steel plate by hand. We did not have shears or gas in those days. The chap helping me left after the plate was cut, to go shooting pigeons. I told him to drop off three or four in my hut as he went past. The pigeons were there by the hundreds and no license was required to shoot them.
>
> I was working all on my own now and just had to drill twelve holes in the plate and bolt it on. But when I took the old plate off I found there was an enormous recess behind it, all filled up and jam-packed with crushed quartz.

One of the lower-level entrances to the Golden Blocks mine. It was here that Charlie had the opportunity to steal a fortune in gold, with practically no risk of being caught. However, he was the sort of man whose conscience would never have given him a moment's rest if he had yielded to the temptation, so it is probably just as well that he did not!

I had been panning gold since I was six years old, so I filled up a gold dish and panned it off. Just imagine my surprise when I discovered that I had three or four ounces of gold! The further I got down into that recess, the more there was. It took me three hours to pan it all off. By the time I finished I had a canvas bag with 24 pounds [11 kg] of gold and mercury mixed together.

What would you do? Nobody within three miles knew all that gold was lying there. It just belonged to some shareholders in a faraway company in England. They were already rich, I told myself. They wouldn't miss it.

I hefted the bag of bullion outside and stood it against the wall. I went back in, marked the new plate off the old one, centered the holes and started drilling. I had twelve holes to drill and was only half way though the first one when I stopped, went outside and said to myself, "Well, I'll just take it over there and put it in a hole under that tree..."

I went back, finished drilling that hole and the next one, and then decided I would put it in a different place in a little cave up the hill. No, that would not do either. So I drilled a couple more holes, went outside; it was a beautiful sunny day. I decided I would put the gold in some old workings that had finished fifteen years before. I drilled some more holes. No, better put it down the track where I would not have so far to come and get it. The last hole drilled. There was a coal seam we used to get the coal for the boiler. I would put it in the old tunnel there and come and get it later on. I finished the plate, bolted it on, cleaned up where I had been working and locked the battery up.

Then I took the gold straight up to the shift boss before I could let myself do anything I might regret. I was too afraid to do anything dishonest. I even had to walk a mile back up nine hundred feet of zig-zag track, then half a mile to his hut, sweating under thousands of pounds' worth of gold.

I arrived just as he was getting ready to have tea. He said, "Why did you come this way?"

I told him that I thought he might want the key to the battery.

"Oh," he said, "you could have bought it along in the morning. Well, you might just as well stay and have tea."

I had a good wash and sat down and ate with him. Afterwards while we were washing up, he asked," By the way, did you find any gold when you were fixing the box?"

I said "Oh yeah, a couple of ounces."

He said, "I told the old man there wouldn't be much. What did you do with it?"

I said, "It's in that bag by the door."

He thought that I had tools in the bag. Well, he went to pick it up and what a shock he got. He was a very religious man, a good chap as well; neither smoked nor drank.

The first thing he said to me was, "Why didn't you pinch it?"

I said, "Don't worry, I hid it in a dozen places in my mind but brought it along just the same."

Now he was even more scared than me: "What am I going to do with it? Did you tell anyone that you had got this? Some of the men here would knife me for half of that ..."

I told him nobody knew, and there was only one thing to do. We took it to the blacksmith shop where there was a set of scales and I told him to weigh it, which he did. He wrote down the weight on two pieces of paper and both of us signed them. "You keep one and I will keep the other," I said. "This is the best way to do it. Now give the bag to me."

Under the bellows in the workshop I kept three bags of silver sand for welding steel drills. I took the middle bag out, put the bag of gold in between the other two and threw a shovelful of coal dust over the lot. I said, "Leave it there. Only you and I know there's a bag of gold there. Just leave the door open. I'm going home."

Next morning there was a meeting of 12 miners, myself and the shift boss in the shop. We were talking for half an hour in the shop and not one of them noticed anything out of the ordinary. But the shift boss was still very jittery and jumpy. He said to me, "Those miners saw that gold. They were looking at it!" He was just imagining it. In fact it stayed there until the Tuesday night when the manager returned from Collingwood and put it into the safe. And so ended my best chance ever to get rich quickly.

Miners at Golden Blocks.

The Golden Blocks was a relatively safe mine underground but Charlie recalled a nasty experience when a bucket of quartz was being hauled up by winch while they were sinking a hole in a particularly rugged and remote spot. The wire broke and the bucket landed on a miner's leg, breaking it just below the knee. They had to carry the 95-kg miner 12 miles up and down hills along a very narrow track. A team of 16 men working four at a time laboured long and hard to get their mate to safety. With some understatement Charlie recorded, "I was very pleased when we finally got him on to a truck."

Down in the mine all the drilling was done by hand. One miner held the drill while the other hit it with a hammer: "When I took the job I didn't know how to sharpen or temper a miner's drill off the hammer but one of the miners showed me. At first it took me three or four minutes just to sharpen one. After a week I could do 12 in 15 minutes."

The mine also used a lot of gelignite, which was packed in by horses, three cases at a time, one on each side of the saddle and one on top, lashed round with a surcingle. One day a packhorse slipped and rolled down the hill about 30 metres. Everybody expected to see the horse and "gelly" go off, but the old horse got back on to its feet at the bottom, none the worse for its experience.

> I worked at the mine for six months. The day I left there the old mine manager took me into a part of the mine where two miners were working on a very rich face, and told me to help myself. I filled a 10lb [4.5 kg] Bell tea tin with specimens that I wanted. So that's how I finished up there. It was quite a good experience for a young feller.

The Golden Blocks mine closed only a few years later, in 1913, having yielded 870 kg of gold over 16 years. Charlie's little hoard of about 11 kg certainly was a significant portion of the mine's total production.

CHAPTER 7

Nelson, Blenheim and the *Penguin* wreck

Moving to Nelson, Charlie joined H Battery, which he enjoyed. They used to drill twice a week, and then had a fortnight in camp every year. He also did more bike racing and swimming and became extremely fit:

> We had a very large section in The Wood, where we had a gymnasium with horizontal bar, springboard, 15-lb [6.8 kg] shot, boxing gloves, punch ball and a racing bike hung up to the rafters so it would not move anywhere. Did you ever try getting on to a bike, strapping your feet on and nothing to drive but the wheel, spinning in the air? I can tell you, the first ten minutes is enough for a start. We all got fairly good at all the games. My younger brother could walk on his hands two lengths of a football field without a spill, and turn a somersault while walking on the footpath. Personally, I could never get the proper balance to walk on my hands.
>
> I raced with Dick and Jack Arnst and George Sutherland four or five years. I was never much good at the game, was quite a fair second-class rider. The fastest time I ever rode was a mile [1.62 km] in 2 minutes and 2/5ths of a second, on Trafalgar Park in 1906. I thought I had won it but I was only fourth.

These keen bike racers had an intense training regime:

> First thing in the morning, a cup of tea or coffee, slice of bread. Pick up your racing bike, put on your shoulders, get

> on your roadster and off down to the track … run round the track at a modest speed, skipping 1,000 or more, then on the bike, have a good look all over it, tie your feet on to the pedals, then go round the track at just a moderate pace until you got warm … We also used to do quite a bit of road riding for exercise. On Sundays three of us used to leave Nelson after breakfast and ride to Blenheim. We had to go round the Tuamarina/Spring Creek way as there was no bridge over the Wairau River near Renwick in those days. We would have a cold bath, rub down, have dinner, walk round for half a hour, then ride back to Nelson [a total of more than 250 km], do [another 16 km] round Trafalgar track, have a cold shower and rub down, then go home for tea. After tea we might walk down to Tahuna and back, call it a day, go to bed.

The Nelson Motor Bus Company was formed around about that time, and Charlie went to work for them. They had two Dennis buses, one a double-decker, but nobody seemed to know much about they worked. They used an accumulator ignition system, which meant they could not charge their own batteries while driving. The bus would leave the Masonic Hotel corner with a fresh battery to go to Tahuna and sometimes need four batteries to get back again.

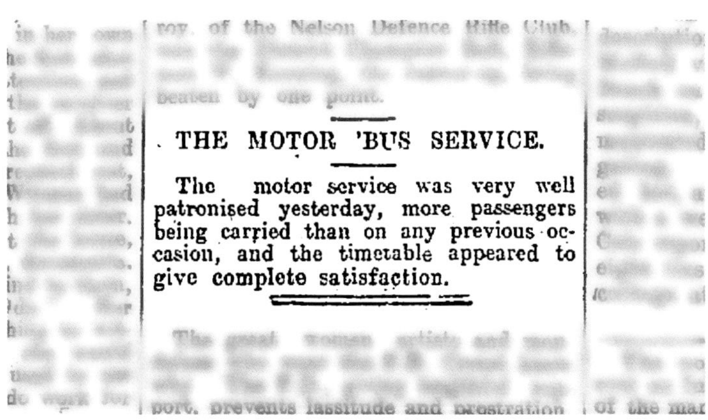

THE MOTOR 'BUS SERVICE.

The motor service was very well patronised yesterday, more passengers being carried than on any previous occasion, and the timetable appeared to give complete satisfaction.

An excerpt from *The Nelson Evening Mail*, Tuesday, February 2, 1909.

At this time the world champion cyclist, a black American named Marshall "Major" Taylor, visited Australia and New Zealand, competing in local events everywhere. Taylor had turned professional in 1896 at the age of 18 and soon emerged as the "most formidable racer in America", but was much discriminated against because of his colour. This did not stop him from winning the world championship in 1899 and establishing seven world records in six weeks. One of his biggest supporters was President Theodore Roosevelt, who took an interest in Taylor throughout his 17-year racing career.

Taylor started in Auckland and went everywhere in NZ where there was a bike race. With him was a man named "Plugger" Bill Martin, another champion cyclist of Irish birth, who had also won many cycling events in Australia but now retired from racing and was following him around on a motor

Marshall "Major" Taylor, an American cyclist who held world championships and visited New Zealand while Charlie was bike racing.

'Plugger' Bill Martin (USA) toured New Zealand with two motor-paced racing cycles, one battery powered and one steam powered.
In Christchurch, he had mechanical problems and was beaten by local hero George Sutherland.

bike – possibly the first in NZ. He rode all the way south to Bluff and then sold the bike to a chap in Christchurch so he would not have to take it back to America. The new owner ran his new motorbike over a fence and broke his neck.

> The bike was up for sale and nobody wanted it so I brought it, and what fun I had. I got more training pushing that bike to start it than I got pedaling any other bike. It had a single-cylinder engine, handlebars about 3 ft 6 inches long, no exhaust, compression lift, accumulator ignition and a vaporiser, not a carburettor like the bikes have today. The engine was 5 ¼ inch bore, 6 ½ inch stroke, with a green hide belt and a mudguard just clear of the back tyre, so the man you were pacing could run his front tyre right up against you without damaging the back wheel. I had the bike about twelve months when a Triumph came out. I had a look at the magneto and carburettor, sent to Wellington and got them both for my bike. After this I had no more trouble.

The bus company went into liquidation so Charlie went to Blenheim with three mates to go harvesting and earn some money quickly. They traveled to Picton on the steamer *Penguin* in third class, right up in the bow. When they got near French Pass one of the sailors was rigging a staging on the deck so the Salvation Army could film Pelorus Jack, the famous dolphin that used to follow ships between the

The Picton viaduct with Picton township in the background. *Photo by NC Winstanley. Courtesy of RN Winstanley.*

Pass and Admiralty Bay. It was a beautiful day, fine with no wind, and Pelorus Jack stayed with the ship for about five miles. Two months later Charlie saw the film of it at a movie theatre.

Pelorus Jack, the famous Risso's dolphin that used to accompany ships travelling through Admiralty Bay to French Pass.

Charlie said he narrowly escaped being on board the *Penguin* shortly afterwards when the ship was wrecked in Cook Strait. Maybe it was just a good story, but as he told it, in February 1909 he and his cobbers had just finished the harvest season in Blenheim so they decided to have a trip to Wellington. This would be a bit of an adventure for a group of country boys. They decided to catch the steamer when she called into Picton on her circuit between Nelson and Wellington. They would go on the 5:30 pm sailing on Friday the 12th. They whiled away the day playing billiards in Blenheim, intending to catch the 4 pm train to Picton, but Charlie got sidetracked by some girls. He became separated from his friends and didn't show up at the station. When the train came the boys decided to let it go without them, and went back into town to find him.

They found Charlie playing cock-of-the-walk in a tearooms, telling tall stories to a group of gigging girls, with his billiards partner. Nobody was too bothered about missing the boat: they could go tomorrow or the next day. They booked into the Masonic Hotel and Charlie managed to get one of the girls to come back for the night, sneaking her up the fire escape to his room because only married couples could book in legitimately. (Incidents like this make me wonder just how many people out there I might be related to!)

A couple of days later a chap passing remarked to him, "Bad disaster, that wreck."

Charlie said, "What wreck?"

The chap told him the *Penguin* had sunk and quite a number of people had been lost. Charlie couldn't believe it. As soon as his head stopped spinning he hopped along to the *Express* office and got a paper. There it was: the whole story, with a photo of the *Penguin* on page one.

Charlie ran back to the hotel and showed the paper to the others, who were having breakfast. After they got over the initial excitement of their close shave they realised that

In 1895 the *Penguin* initiated regular ferry sailings between Lyttelton and Wellington. Fourteen years later, while running between Picton and Wellington, she sank with the loss of 72 lives.

the girl who had waylaid Charlie had saved all their lives. They all wanted to meet her, but Charlie knew that the fuss and attention this would generate would do nothing for his reputation so he said she had already left town. Soon one of them began singing a popular song of the time, "Thank God for a girl like you."

The circumstances of the *Penguin* wreck were pitiful, with 72 lives lost after the ship collided with a rock or possibly floating debris in bad weather at night and sank near Cape Terawhiti, the southwest corner of the North Island. All the lifeboats were capsized after they were launched so the women and children, who'd been given priority, came off worst. Only 14 of the 46 passengers survived, with just one woman among them.

It's interesting to speculate how Charlie and his mates might have come off if they had been on the ship. Certainly Charlie was a strong and fit man and an excellent swimmer, but who knows what difference that would have made when being cast ashore on a rocky coast by massive waves?

Bruce E. Collins, in his book *The Wreck of the Penguin*, lists two people who missed the connecting train and were saved by missing the ferry that fateful night. He doesn't have Charlie's story.

CHAPTER 8

Blenheim and the *Echo*

After their near escape from the *Penguin* disaster Charlie and his mates did not go north. He stayed in Blenheim and found work overhauling two double-decker Thorneycroft buses that belonged to a Mr. Lindstroum. He recalled that by taking the tops off, the buses could also be used for carting wheat and barley.

Then he went on a fishing boat to get experience with small oil engines. They trawled out of the Wairau Bar, the small river mouth port of Blenheim. He recalled later that the fishing was much better in those days. Small trawlers used to do mostly day-trips fishing Cloudy Bay and Clifford Bay, catching wetfish for the local market. After that he went to Parker's garage in Blenheim overhauling and doing all kinds of car work, though there were only about six cars in Blenheim at the time. Parker bought a Sidley car and put him on driving it as a service car. When not driving it he had work building stationary oil engines.

Charlie was proud of his 'number eight wire" skills and recorded this story of doing a tricky repair to a car with a broken axle. It happened when he drove a man down to Kaikoura to buy some sheep from various farms along the coast road. Just north of Kaikoura they had to be towed through the Hapuku River:

> There were no bridges across the roads then, and it was just after a big flood. The team that towed us through was of four

bullocks. I took the magneto off to keep it dry and away we went, but in about the middle of the river the car fell off a great big boulder and dropped about four feet. When we got to the other side and on to the road again I put the magneto back and started the car up, only to find when I tried to put it into first gear that none of the gears would work. I told the bullock driver to haul the car to the side of the road, then jacked it up and put fence posts under it. When I removed the differential I found that the right-hand wheel had sheared off right ... There was nothing more I could do so I borrowed a sulky from a nearby farm, drove into Kaikoura and went to the first blacksmith shop I could find. He told me I would have to wait a fortnight if I could not get it welded. He said that he would not take the job on.

I asked him if he had any mild steel axles for a sulky, and when he said that he did, I asked him to lend me a forge and a striker and said I'd do the job myself. I welded it, swaged a square and put a round for the thread, straightened it as near as I could measure on the flat sheet and left the weld fairly thick so that it could be turned on the lathe when I got to Blenheim. Then took it back, fitted it and was able to drive the car into Kaikoura that night. Later, when I got back to Blenheim, Mr. Birch put it in the lathe, hit it two or three times with a hammer, and it was fixed, in fact it remained in use until the car was scrapped.

A bullock team crossing the Hapuku River. From this picture it is perhaps not so surprising that Charlie had difficulty driving a car through.

Charlie continued to enjoy his sporting activities in Blenheim. While working for Parker he joined the local rowing club. He used to take his own rowing skiff down to the Wairau Bar on a Sunday with two other men who used to take a pair. They would have a swim, have dinner and row back again. When a flood broke through the protecting wall and filled Blenheim with water and the shops with silt, he rowed the skiff into all the hotels – "The water in the Royal Hotel was over the billiard table."

Men were expected to wear swimsuits with a bib up the front in those days, and anything else was a bit improper. Charlie was too casual and it nearly earned him a charge of indecent exposure while performing another rescue:

> I always used to row the skiff in a swimsuit and drop the top part and tie it around my waist so that I could get some more of a suntan. One day I was about half a mile down from the rowing shed when I saw a little girl on the shore, howling. I asked her what was the matter and she told me her little brother had fallen in the river. I jumped over the side of the skiff, had a look along the bottom for about 30 feet, came up, got a breath, went down again and managed to find the little fellow. I grabbed him and hit out for the shore, told the little girl to show me where they lived and to run. I kept turning the boy upside down and upright again while I was running to his home. His mother got panicky so I got hot water and put him in it after I got him breathing, put him in hot blankets

Opawa River, Blenheim.

> and put him in a cot that was there and told the woman to keep him warm. The boy survived his ordeal and the rescue. When went back to the river my skiff had drifted downstream and was on the other side, so I swam across, towed it to the bank where I could empty it out, and finished my row.
> That night the paper had a piece in it about me knocking about indecently exposed. I went to the newspaper office and explained that I was carrying a boy half drowned and taking him home, and that my togs were tied at the waist. Anyhow, they printed an apology in the next issue.

After the Blenheim swimming baths were opened in December 1910 Charlie put on several demonstrations of "long diving" (though he complained that they never had a decent height to go from). Advertisements for these events described him as "New Zealand's Amateur Long-diving Champion". A report in the *Marlborough Express* of 16 November 1911 mentioned one of his performances at a "gaslight gala": "The evening's amusement opened with an exhibition of swimming every known stroke by Mr Bert Carpenter, after which Mr Charles Jacobsen gave a display of aquatic feats, his high and long diving being very meritorious ... the 50 yds sprint resulted in a tie between C. Jacobsen and S. Simson."

But on this occasion Charlie wasn't quite the star of the show: "The programme was brought to a close by the thrill of the evening in Mr Carpenter's demon fire and fireworks act ... enveloped in a sack flaming with methylated spirit and kerosene, he turned a complete somersault from the lofty staging into the baths below."

There was however another side to Charlie Jacobsen. He could be a bit free with his fists:

> One day a young chap got into difficulties while swimming across the river. Two others went to his assistance but they could not manage him so almost everybody yelled out, "Go and get him, Charley", which I did. I no sooner had him ashore than a chap trying to be smart said, "You'll get another medal for that!" I just hauled him off, gave him a straight left, told him that you never saved a person for a medal, but to save their life."

The rescue, but not the punch, was reported in the local paper: "It is firmly believed that but for Mr Jacobsen's timely aid the boy would have been drowned."

Charlie also took on football but broke an ankle in a practice game. When he came out of hospital the doctor advised him to take on a light job, because the concrete floor in the garage would be too hard. He took a job driving for a local businessman, a Mr Vavasour, for six months. Then went back to sea again. This marked the beginning of the period during which Charlie permanently switched to being a seafarer. He worked as engineer on a number of coastal ships, starting with the *Echo.* He also served on the *Magic* and the *Omaha,* all of which were owned by Captain Eckford.

On his first trip Charlie soon managed to get into a fight:

> When we arrived at Karamea the captain, Fred MacIntyre, and I and were having a drink with the boss of the local hotel when three sawmill hands came along. They had been drinking all day. I used to wear plus fours and stockings for biking. The fashion was a small bun hat. I did not look very heavy but weighed [78 kg]. We had been talking a little when one of the sawmill hands knocked my bun hat off. I just looked at him and picked it up again. No sooner had I turned my back than he knocked it off again, so I said to him, " Don't do that again or I might get annoyed."
>
> The boss of the hotel said to me in a very quiet voice, "That chap is the champion of all the sawmills here," but I knew he could not really be much good because if he was, he wouldn't go behind your back to hit anybody.
>
> Although I had my back to him I could see him in the mirror in front of me, so as he went to knock my hat off again I grabbed his wrist and sat down quickly. He went over my head and landed in a heap. I was facing him when he got up, and he made a haymaker swipe at me but I sidestepped. I told him I did not fight in a hotel and always used gloves in an argument. He thought I was frightened to fight him bare-knuckled and called me all kinds of names. So I invited him out into the paddock behind the hotel and told him that I would fight six 2-minute rounds, the boss of the hotel to referee, and kicking and biting banned. We took off our coats and squared up.
>
> Well, he drew his right fist back but my left went straight out

The steamer *Kairaki* and the *Echo* at Gilbert's wharf, Karamea. Today the port of Karamea is too silted up for navigation owing to the huge amounts of sediment loosened up by the Murchison earthquake of 1929.

The scow *Echo* docked in the Opawa River, Blenheim.

> as his right came round. I ducked and gave him two in the tummy, knocked him off his feet. When he got up he charged straight at me with his head down, expecting to get me in the stomach. I sidestepped and gave him a right uppercut that caught him on the eye. He turned, I waded in and gave him right and left in the stomach. That finished the fight. He didn't know the first thing about fighting, was just used to bluffing all the others. He apologised and we all went and had a drink. After that he never bullied anybody again.

In January 1911 Charlie was in Karamea when a large scow, the *Zingara,* ran ashore after a sudden change of weather while being towed out of the harbour with a big load of timber for Sydney. The vessel washed northwards along the beach for about a mile but was undamaged. An operation was mounted to refloat her but even with the scow's donkey engine and a geared winch, powerful enough to snap an 8-cm rope, they could not shift her. The problem was to get an anchor that would hold while the ship was winched towards it. On a sandy beach the ship stuck firmly while the anchors pulled out without holding.

A local farmer named O'Connor reckoned he could make an anchor that would be strong enough to break any of their ropes, and Charlie introduced him to the captain, Adolph Somers, who told them to go ahead. They assembled a frame using a number of 15 x 15-cm baulks of green timber, which cost almost nothing in those days. They tied a big steel hawser round the middle, then at low tide towed it with horses as far down the beach as possible and piled about 30 bags of sand on top. As the tide rose the wooden frame gradually sank into the sand, leaving the piece of hawser as a very strong anchorage point. At high tide they were able to haul the vessel against this, although it took four days to pull it back to the harbour entrance. The vessel was successfully refloated a month after she stranded, and they never had to unload any of the cargo.

In May 1912 Charlie took cargo from Wellington to Gisborne, then went on to Great Barrier Island to load kauri timber for Lyttelton. They were only lightly ballasted. There were seven scows and a schooner in Gisborne at the

The *Zingara*, aground at Karamea in 1911. Charlie witnessed the incident and the successful refloating of the vessel, which was due to the ingenuity of a local farmer.

time, and after a few drinks the skippers decided to have a race to the Barrier as they were all going there anyway. Only one of the other vessels had an auxiliary engine, so each of the engineers gave his word only to use the engines in an emergency or when going about.

> Just before we got to East Cape we ran into a hard northwest wind. The other ships anchored to wait it out but our skipper had sailed around Cape Horn half a dozen times and decided to beat around the Cape. While we were standing in for Mayor Island after we got round the Cape, blowing fairly stiff, the skipper said, "Take in your outer and inner jib. Take a reef in the main and mizzen." I wondered why and asked him. He replied, If you see it come clear in the north when it's still blowing northwest and raining, you need to get some of the canvas stowed." He was right. In about 20 minutes it came away from the north and I thought the sticks would go out of her. It only lasted about half an hour and then the wind came away from the west and we hauled right up to Great Barrier Island. I only used the engines to get alongside the wharf.

The scow *Echo* berthed in Wellington Harbour.

We loaded up and had quite a nice trip back with the northwest still blowing so it was a fair wind right down to Lyttelton. We were home and unloaded before any of the others even arrived at Great Barrier.

After unloading the ship went up for survey, which meant pulling the engines apart, drawing the tail shaft and making general repairs to the hull and rigging. When we came off the slip, the ship was fumigated and we all had to stay ashore for 48 hours. The captain, mate and myself stayed at the Majestic Hotel while the crew stayed at some of the other hotels.

The *Echo* used to have a 64-gallon [288 litre] benzine (petrol) tank on deck, while the rest of the ship's fuel was carried on deck in cases, stacked forward. Each case contained two 4-gallon [18.2 litre] cans, a very hazardous cargo. I asked the fitter from Anderson's foundry, who was doing the engines, to close the valve from the fuel tanks as I had to go ashore; this was about 4.40 in the afternoon. I did the business I had to do, went to the hotel, had a shave and a bath, went up to Christchurch and saw Fuller's Vauderville Entertainment and got back to the hotel about 11 pm.

First thing in the morning I opened the cabin doors and smelt benzine. To air the ship out I opened the engine doors and skylight and lifted four hatches off each side. Then I told the mate and the cook and all the crew that six cases of benzine had run out of the tanks during the night. I didn't tell the captain, as he was ashore.

The foundry man and I were down into the engine room fixing up the port engine, so we didn't see the skipper and the shipwright, Mr Miller, go down to the engine room. In front of the starboard engine was a sounding well and they had come to see how much water the ship had made during the night. It was dark so one of them struck a match to see. There was a big explosion and the floor and all the hatches that were left on blew up into the air. The first explosion blew out the bulkhead between the engine room and the hold. Then a second explosion blew out the cabin floor, engine room skylight and the entire floor in the engine room, carried away the forward bulkhead and set everything alight.

The fitter dived past the bulkhead and got out on the port side. I made a dive for the ladder on the starboard side but there was no ladder there. I jammed my leg between the starboard shaft and long stringer but eventually scrambled out with both arms burnt and face scorched a bit.

Like other coastal scows that plied the waters around New Zealand, the *Echo* was a fine sight under sail. *Photo courtesy Picton Museum.*

Initially a fire party from the *Terra Nova*, which was berthed alongside, tried to put out the fire with chemical fire extinguishers but these were not up to the job. Soon the fire brigade came and used four hydrants to keep the blaze under control until the petrol burnt out. The water filled her up over the engines and there was £50 worth of damage.

The *Terra Nova* was the polar explorer Captain Scott's ship, recently back from picking up the survivors of the ill-fated expedition. Charlie became acquainted with a number of the crew and one of them, Charles Williams, came to work on the *Echo*. Charlie recorded that

> He gave me a suit of clothes that they wore down there, also a book that they read when one lot of them got broken away from the main camp. The name of the book was *David Copperfield*. The reason I accepted it from him was I thought he might give it to some barmaid, so I sent it home to my mother to look after. About six months later he got a letter from the Dickens Fellowship Society, London, telling him it was worth its weight in gold if he would sell it. He came to me and said, "Read this."
> I said, as a joke, "What a pity! My mother burnt it, thought it was old junk."
> "Oh well, never mind," he said," I suppose I would have given it away anyway."

> I wrote home, got my mother to send it to me by registered post, then made Williams take it to the bank and send it to England. I think he got £500 for it.

In 1913 there was a widespread strike throughout New Zealand. For some reason about six small ships, including the *Echo*, were able to take a cargo of foodstuffs to Hokitika, where all arrived at about the same time. Charlie's job when the ship was tied up for loading and unloading was to see that the winch was in good order and that the engine was ready for sea. The rest of the time he could do what he liked.

There were half a dozen other young men with jobs like his who also had time off so they rented a car and explored.

When the captain was ashore it was the mate's job to see that the cargo was unloaded and the ship loaded with timber. This led to some resentment and another fight, much worse this time:

> With all the ships in it was hard to get wharf labour and the longer it took the more fun we young chaps had and the nearer the strike would be to finishing when we got back to Wellington. Now the mate had a Foreign Going Master's certificate and was a big Swede, weighed about 15 stone [95 kg], but could not get a ship of his own as he had knocked a

Hokitika Wharf lay alongside the town, at the mouth of the Hokitika River. The port was notoriously treacherous. *Photo courtesy Hocken Snapshop.*

Hokitika Wharf around 1900.

cook out on one ship and put a boot into his ribs after. I don't think he was aware that I knew about this.

One night when I came home to the ship the mate went off the handle and told me that I had said to the skipper that he was loafing instead of getting the timber on. This was untrue, in fact I hadn't even seen the skipper since he went ashore and we all had been up to Greymouth in the car.

The mate called me all the names he could think of and some of them no man would take from a foreigner. I said, "Mister, you will have to apologise for that or I will jam it down your throat." He only laughed; he was relying on his weight so I hit him a flat-hander on the face and had my coat off in less than a second as I knew that smack would make him mad. He got up and if I had stopped the haymaker that he sent after me that would have been the finish, but I ducked and it went over my head. I gave him four or five rights to the solar plexus, side-stepped and as he rushed me I side stepped again, hit him behind the ear and knocked him into his cabin, where I knew I could wallop him so long as I kept out of his reach. Then he reached up and turned the light off. I thought to myself, "He's going to have a go in the dark," though there was some light shining through the skylight from the wharf.

He dived back into his cabin and I heard something go click. I thought he had put on a knuckle duster so quickly I went forward to the forecastle where there were five seamen and said to them, "Lend me that lamp, and come along to see fair play. Don't interfere, but if he knocks me out just stop him from putting the boot in." So I went in front carrying the lamp, and had six steps to go down the companionway. I was just putting the lamp on the table when one of the sailors said, "Look out, Chief!" The Swede had a knife. My left hand shot across my stomach and my right hand over my face and I got stabbed right in the palm of my left hand. I grabbed his wrist and sat down quicker than you can read this, then the sailors grabbed him. I said to them, "One hold the lamp, one stand in each doorway. Now don't interfere." I hit the Swede until he couldn't stand up, then sat him in the corner and punched him some more until he yelled for mercy, then wiped my bleeding hand all over his best suit.

I tried to stop the blood by wrapping a couple of towels round and then went to find a doctor. The only place I could find open was the printing office. I walked in, found one chap working and asked him could I get a doctor. When he asked what happened I told him I'd fallen on a broken bottle. He took me along to Dr Feldman (a German who had been in New Zealand long enough to be naturalised), who asked me what had happened and I said two or three of us were skylarking and I fell on a bottle. His nurse came in, took off the towels and the chap with me almost fainted when he saw the mess. The nurse washed my hand and the doctor put six stitches in it. After he was finished, he said in a very quiet voice, "Those Norwegian knives are sharp ..." It had been one of those folding knives and I think it was only hearing the click of the spring that saved my life.

I said to the doctor, "How much do I owe you?" He said, "Thirty shillings." I paid him and said, "If I knock them all out again in the morning, will you sew me up again?" He said, I'll do it for nothing, give him hell!"

I stayed ashore that night and next morning went down before breakfast, taking an officer off another ship with me. I said to the mate, "You will apologise to me in front of the crew or come ashore to the boxing clubrooms and fight it like a man or I'll have you charged for attempted murder."

After this incident the crew refused to sail with him and the captain of the west coast mail boat said he would come up as mate if I would go as engineer on the mail boat running to south Westland. It was a semi-diesel job so I agreed.

When we arrived in Wellington we were all paid off and I went back to Hokitika. So the strike didn't affect me much but you can still see the scar where the knife cut my hand.

CHAPTER 9

World War 1

Charlie was still working as engineer on coastal ships on 4 August 1914 when Britain declared war against Germany. As soon as Charlie's ship came into port and he heard the news, he was straight into the Hokitika Army recruiting office, at 1 pm on 17 August. There was his duty to serve the country and he wasn't going to miss out on any opportunity for adventure that might come with it. He also knew that he already had the necessary experience to go in the first detachment because he had been in the Takaka Mounted Rifles and H Battery, Nelson.

Charlie recalled that in all, 73 men immediately volunteered in Hokitika but only 17 including himself passed "A" Grade. His induction medical described him as "height 5' 8" [1.73 m] weight 151 lb [69 kg] chest 34/38in [85/95 cm], religion RC, tattoo on left fore arm." He became Private Jacobsen, No. 6/658, in the 1st Canterbury Infantry Battalion. This was the beginning of nearly five years' service in four theatres of war.

Unfortunately, like many soldiers of that era Charlie did not record much of his experiences and telling his story is largely a matter of piecing together the threads from his military record (which is short on detail and sometimes contradictory) and other sources that describe what his units did and when. Tellingly, he wrote less about the war as it progressed, so that the most we know about (though it is still not much) is his induction, training and the long sea journey to Egypt.

Now the fun started. We left Hokitika the next morning for Christchurch by train, picked up about 20 more men from Greymouth and Westport. The Otira tunnel was not through the hill then so we marched from the station to meet coaches at the bottom of Arthur's Pass. Arriving in Christchurch we marched to the barracks at Addington. My mother was staying with my younger brother Walter about 100 yards off the road where we were marching along. I asked permission to drop in and say goodbye to her as I had not seen her for over two years, but they would not let me. We arrived at the barracks in Addington that night and were allotted the tents that we had to stay in during training. The next day we were attached to the North Canterbury Division as the 13th North Canterbury and Westland Regiment, which was composed of North Canterbury and west coast men.

Charlie ready to go, 1914.

The Canterbury Contingent of the New Zealand Expeditionary Force at the Sockbum Camp, 1914.

At Addington it rained almost every day for a week and the place became so muddy they decided to shift us to Sockburn. We marched up there and the ground was good, sort of shingle, the rain did not stay on top but just soaked through. They didn't give us very much in the way of training because we had already been through it all in the Volunteers. Mainly the training was in rifle shooting. I passed A Grade, which was no surprise since I had had a rifle since I was a boy of 12.

Charlie recorded with some resentment that the enlisted men did not get any leave at night from camp:

The day before we left Christchurch to join our ship in Lyttelton they gave us leave from 2 to 6 pm, which allowed the Christchurch boys to say goodbye to their family and friends but wasn't much use to the rest of us. That was all the leave we got except on the day we left New Zealand from Wellington. So once we enlisted, for most of us that was the end of our contact with our loved ones. For those who were

Charlie's contingent; Charlie is in the second row from the bottom and third from the left.

The Canterbury Infantry Regiment marching on September 23, 1914, from the Sockburn Camp to the Sockburn Railway Station to board a train for Lyttelton.

> killed on the battlefield, the last time they ever saw their families was the day they enlisted.

Meanwhile, as soon as war had been declared between England and Germany the ship *Athenic*, which had been in the port of Wellington, was requisitioned as a troopship. *Athenic* was designated His Majesty's New Zealand Transport No. 11. She was then dispatched to Lyttelton to collect troops from the south.

In *The New Zealanders at Gallipoli*, Col. Fred Waite described the preparations for war:

> Addington Park became the gathering and training centre for the troops of the Canterbury Military District, being

> first the Canterbury Mounted Rifles Regiment and second the Canterbury Infantry Battalion, made up of the 1st (Canterbury), 2nd (North Canterbury), 12th (Nelson) and [Charlie's unit] the 13th (North Canterbury and Westland) Regiments.
> The territorial system of compulsory training was still in its infancy, but it was considered advisable to retain the territorial distinctions. Each of the four Military Districts was asked to supply one regiment of mounted rifles and one battalion of infantry. Each territorial regiment and battalion supplied to the Expeditionary Force a squadron and a company respectively, and these units retained their badges and the customs of their parent organisations.

On 23 September the *Athenic* took the troops on board and sailed to Wellington, where she stayed until 16 October. Her departure was delayed by concerns about German raiders in the Pacific and Indian oceans. The ships waited for Australian and Japanese warships to accompany them. (It's surprising to realise that the Japs were on our side in World War 1.)

Athenic at Queens Wharf, Wellington.

Sorting kit-bags alongside the *Athenic*, Lyttelton. *Courtesy of F.W. Randall.*

Charlie noted the number 13 of his regiment and also recorded that when the *Athenic* left New Zealand his bunk was 13. "I would probably not have come back from the war if I'd been more superstitious."

They had to undergo more training in Wellington. "We had about three weeks there, route marching, shooting at Trentham and a skirmish or two in the hills up the back of the city." He was unimpressed by the army's organisation and equipment:

> Just imagine trying to climb over the hills with light boots with no nails in them. You would go up a step or two then slide back down. After a while they got a bit more sense and gave us better boots.
>
> The day we left New Zealand they gave us the afternoon off but we had to be back on board by 9 o'clock. The 13th

Charlie's contingent at Trentham. Charlie is not in this photo.

An impressive Sunday service on the *Athenic*. *Courtesy of F.W. Randall.*

Company were accommodated at the bottom of the ship's No. 1 hold, right up close to the bow. It was all right for anybody who had been to sea, but not too good for the new chums.

When it was time to go we just walked on; there was no send-off or anything like they had later on. We pulled out into the stream and they picked a few of us out to act as military police and they went ashore and rounded up out the rest of the boys who'd missed the ship. We stayed at anchor for a day or two then left for Australia, where Hobart was the first stop.

They spent the first day or two at sea fixing up the training that had to be done on the voyage. Eight of the men, including Charlie, volunteered to clean out the mess every morning, which freed them from any Army duty.

Our ships arrived in Hobart and they decided to give us a route march round the town. We used to march in fours in those days. We fell in and marched like old soldiers, all in step. They gave us the "march easy" command and the Hobart girls gave us apples and oranges and fell in among us so we were five or six, a girl in between. When we were very nearly back to Hobart, still "marching easy", who should be standing on the side of the road but General Godley, our O.C. [officer commanding]. We never saw him until we were

Departure from Lyttelton of the First Contingent, 2NZEF on the troopship *Dunera* on January 5 1915, when the 20th Battalion embarked for the voyage to Egypt.

very nearly alongside, too late to call us to attention. We had to do an hour's pack drill every day on board for a week but we didn't mind.

After that we weren't allowed ashore, not anybody, even if they had relations. Two boys with us had their mothers living in Hobart and applied for an hour to go and say goodbye, but they could not get a permit. I and four of my cobbers thought this was bloody unfair as we knew what it felt like going away without saying goodbye to your mother, knowing perfectly well that you might never come back. So we waited until dark then we lowered them both over the bow onto the wharf and told them we would keep watch for them until 11 o'clock. They were just boys, volunteers going to war for the glory, adventure and to fight for their country. We took turn about to watch until they came back, then hauled them on board again. But they never got to fight, and their mothers never saw them again. Both boys were killed in the hail of machine gun fire from the Turks on the higher ground as they went up the beach at Gallipoli – they probably never even fired a shot themselves.

> We went ashore again at Perth, where we joined up with the Australian fleet. It was quite a sight to see them all in line with our escorts on both sides plus one in front and seven behind. The voyage was very monotonous. Each morning we would get up, do physical jerks, wash and shave, then have breakfast, then the company did signalling and other stuff. We went below, cleaned out, then had boxing until dinnertime. I must say the food was very good but sometimes spoiled by some of the cooks.

Soon after leaving Perth Charlie and his compatriots were nearly witnesses to a famous naval skirmish in which the German cruiser *Emden* was destroyed by one of the escorting Australian warships. When they were passing the Cocos Islands they had a moment of excitement as the warship *Sydney* came from ahead right through the convoy and headed off at full speed. She had just received a message that a strange warship had been sighted at Direction Island, just 55 miles away. It was the first bit of real excitement they'd had on the voyage. They did not see or hear the action, but after a few hours received the news that the *Sydney* had sunk the *Emden* (in fact the captain had run his damaged ship aground to avoid sinking) and was on her way back to join the convoy. Four days later the *Sydney* caught up with the rest of the convoy just after it arrived at Colombo in Ceylon (now Sri Lanka).

Here Charlie had another of his diving experiences. Local boys were diving for threepenny bits and sixpences that the soldiers threw overboard for them. Charlie asked his commanding officer, who had seen him swimming and diving in Hokitika, for permission to go and swim with them. He soon found he could get the coins just as easily as the locals. A coin goes down quite slowly when thrown into water and flutters from side to side as it sinks. Charlie quickly learned the trick of swimming down underneath the coin and looking up where it could be seen quite plainly through the deep, clear water. He gave the coins that he got to some of the "nigger boys", as the Anzacs called the locals.

Then the locals challenged him to a race with their best swimmer, who Charlie described as a well-developed boy of about 17. They agreed to race from the stern of the ship to the bow, a distance of exactly 500 feet [152 m] . At that time Charlie could swim 100 yards [97 m] in 58 seconds so he was pretty confident.

> We both swam slowly towards the stern. He said to me, "You say go." I turned when we got to the stern, hit my feet quick to get them on top, lashed out with my right, said "Go" and got a flying start on him. I went flat out, sure that I would beat him, but just as I got level with the foremast he passed me and went on to win by about 3 feet [1 m]. Well, you should have heard all those boys on deck, "Thought you could swim!", etc, etc. I just yelled back at them, "Come and have a go yourselves!" I shook hands with the other swimmer and told him we had no one in New Zealand that could beat him.
>
> Then he said, "So what are you like at diving?" I replied, "Oh, not so bad." We swam round to the companionway. I told him to wait while I went to the upper deck where all the officers were and asked Lt-Colonel Douglas Macbean Stewart, if we could bring the local boy on board for some high diving. He said, "Yes, go ahead."
>
> So the local boy and I climbed to the top of the bridge wheelhouse and both dived off. We swam back again. This time I said, "Very high dive," and the two of us were soon climbing the rigging on the foremast. He got halfway and said, "I stop here." I went on up, shimmied my way out along the yard and dived off. When I came up he dived off the deck and said to me, "You best diver I seen." This made me feel better for not winning the swimming race!
>
> When we had shore leave in Colombo my new friend took me all round the place and helped us bargain with the locals to make sure we got the things we wanted to buy at the lowest price.

Then on the morning of 17 November the New Zealand transports, escorted by the *Hampshire*, headed once again for the deep water. It was another monotonous voyage with the next stop at Aden, where no one was allowed ashore.
As Waite recalls in *The New Zealanders at Gallipoli*:

> Exactly seven weeks after leaving Wellington Harbour, the lookouts saw with the dawn of December 3, the great white city of Alexandria standing in a sea of mist. Slowly we

> forged ahead until clustering spars resolved themselves into a multitude of transports and captured sailing ships, for here were interned most of the enemy mercantile marine captured in the Eastern Mediterranean.
>
> Soon men and stores, guns and horses, were en route to the railway station, where troop trains were waiting, and in a few hours were speeding across some of the most magnificent agricultural country in the world – the delta of the Nile.
>
> It was decided to use the New Zealand Expeditionary Force as the nucleus of a Division. The New Zealand Infantry Brigade and the New Zealand Mounted Rifles Brigade were to be joined by the 1st Australian Light Horse Brigade and the 4th Australian Infantry Brigade, at that time on the high seas, en route to Egypt.

At first the New Zealanders were based at El-Zaytoun, not far from Cairo, for their training, then sent to the Suez Canal.

Waite recorded that on the afternoon of 25 January the news came from Army Corps Headquarters that the Infantry Brigade was needed urgently on the Suez Canal to support Indian troops against an attack by the advancing Turks. This was perhaps a foolhardy attack, given that the defense of Egypt was strengthened by two great natural obstacles – the Sinai Desert and the chain of salt lakes connected by the Suez Canal. It might be an opportunity to give the Turks a hiding.

Charlie's Company was at El-Ferdan, along with two companies of Sikhs and Gurkhas. "Here we had our first experience of war when the Turks marched right past us and tried to get across at Ferry Post." Four small enemy field guns opened fire, but were quickly put out of action by a few well-directed rounds from HMS *Clio*.

The Nelson Company saw a bit more action, repulsing an amphibious assault in five pontoons. As Waite described it:

> Soon both banks of the Canal were ablaze with the spluttering of rifles fired by soldiers undergoing their baptism of fire. The rival artilleries now came into action, and by dawn the battle raged over the two and a half miles of Canal ... The Turk made attempt after attempt, but our infantry easily accounted for the men in the pontoons; the field artillery scattered the bridge-making squads; and when it was fully light, the ships' guns caused such consternation in the enemy's reserves

> that gradually the attack melted away... The enemy's total casualties were about 3000 in killed, wounded and prisoners. The British loss was 18 killed and 83 wounded.

Only one New Zealander was killed in this action A month later they were moved back to Zeitoun. Meanwhile the forces gathered in Egypt and the landings at Gallipoli were planned. Two Colonial Divisions – the 1st Australian Division and the New Zealand and Australian Division – were designated the Australian and New Zealand Army Corps, or the ANZAC forces as they came to be called.

The story of the 1915 campaign in the Dardanelles has been fully told elsewhere and it is not necessary to go through it again here. However it is interesting to trace Charlie's part in it, as much as we can from the scant details he left. They departed on 12 April for Lamnos and then for Gallipoli on 24 April, landing at Anzac Cove next morning.

Charlie wrote very little about his experiences in this infamous theatre of war though we do know that initially he was among the Canterbury Scouts, "but after the first day or two there was no scouting to do so I was made a sniper."

I have been told this story so many times, especially by my Auntie Phyl who would repeat it to us as Charlie told it to her. This is the gist of what Charlie said and I have tried to put it as close to his own words as possible, to get it as close to what an old man recalls of what was the truth:

> To be a sniper meant sitting still for hours. But a lonely job spending hours on your own and not moving, when you had to move they were slow movements with your eyes everywhere. This day I spotted a German officer and he saw me at the same time, he came running towards me with his Luger pistol out. He got one shot off, just clipping the top of my ear, it did not hurt but there was a bit of blood. He had to climb over a log to get a better shot at me and that's when I lined him up and killed him first shot. If the log hadn't been there it would have been me, not him. There was nobody else around, so I went down to take his pistol as a souvenir. Looking through his wallet I found a letter from his wife. Most of us could read a little bit of German, so I worked my way through it and although I couldn't understand much of

> it, her name and two others were at the bottom. This brought me to tears, I had just killed a man with two children. I wrote to his wife telling her that he died a hero defending his country and that he didn't suffer and how sorry I was. I couldn't say where it came from or my name as we were at war and every letter was censored. The fun went out of sniping after that.

He did bring home a Luger so you can decide for yourself whether this is all true or just a good story. The Luger was in the family for many years until 2011 when it was given to the war museum at Waiouru.

Charlie's Word War 1 Luger, souvenired from a German officer he killed, was an object of endless fascination among us when we were kids.

As will be seen, Charlie's time at Gallipoli was comparatively short owing to illness and wounds, and it is likely that he felt deeply dissatisfied, possibly even ashamed, for missing so much of the action. Nevertheless he was in some of the big events including the 25 April landing at Anzac Cove and the fighting for Walker Ridge, Krithia, and, briefly, Chunuk Bair.

All he recorded about the initial landing was that he was stroke oarsman in the first boat that went ashore from the destroyer *Bulldog* at Anzac Cove. I think the whole battle was so dreadful, plus it was his first experience of real combat, that he didn't feel like saying much more about it. While they were waiting, the ship took two direct hits, killing two naval ratings and wounding three New Zealanders.

HMS Bulldog, 1914.

The second shot went straight though the funnel. Loading troops off a ship into boats was a new thing and some men fell in the water so heavily loaded they went straight to the bottom and drowned. We can hardly begin to imagine the horror of it all.

But that was only the start of a battle that went from bad to worse. Charlie later wrote that ten days after landing at ANZAC Cove the New Zealand Infantry Brigade was deployed south to Cape Helles "to help the Pommy regiments. A couple of days later [on 8 May] we made a daylight attack across a piece of land that afterwards was called the Daisy Patch." Once again he stated just the bare facts, but the truth was much worse. According to the official record, in this event on 8 May 1915 the New Zealand Infantry Brigade suffered 835 casualties for no gain:

> From this front-line trench the Regulars had advanced the day before, but had been driven back. Presently the word was passed along that the New Zealanders would prepare to charge. When some Munsters and Essex saw the preparations, they shouted, "You're not going to charge across the daisy patch, are you?" "Of course we are," the Aucklanders answered. "God help you," they said, and watched with admiration as the New Zealanders flung themselves over the top.
>
> The converging machine-gun fire from the clumps of fir trees swept the ground like a hose. This famous "daisy patch" was situated just to the left of a dry creek-bed running from near the village of Krithia ... a piece of ground about 100 yards across, absolutely devoid of cover.
>
> The troops had hardly got a quarter of the way across the patch when there burst a further terrific storm of machinegun and rifle fire. Heavily laden with entrenching tools and

> equipment, the troops were exhausted and could go no farther. By 3 p.m. the thin line was digging itself in.
> Canterbury had advanced about 250 yards, Auckland had two companies about the same distance, but the right company had fallen back owing to heavy cross machine-gun fire from a clump of fir trees. Wellington had made good about 300 yards, but were under very heavy fire from a Turkish trench on our left front. Two companies of the Otago Regiment were sent in to help Auckland, who had lost heavily ... All that afternoon our men hung on under a withering fire ... This effort had spent itself before 7 pm. The Canterburys had gone forward some 400 yards. The Aucklands went well ahead, but lost very heavily in officers. They fell back almost to their original line. Wellington made a substantial advance, but were held up by the enemy machine guns ...

Now Charlie's part in this becomes tantalisingly interesting, for the record continues:

> At 3.53 p.m. on May 9, an order was received to take over the section from our left to the Krithia Nullah. The 87th Brigade was to go into support, the line being held by the Wellingtons, Otagos, and Canterburys. Part of the 88th Brigade was also retired. The marksmen of the Canterburys took the enemy snipers by surprise, and established a moral superiority over them.

Since Charlie's role was as a marksman, no doubt he contributed to this small success in an otherwise hopeless assault. It was not until 11 May that the New Zealanders were relieved, ending the Battle of Krithia. After barely two weeks on the peninsula, the Brigade had already sustained more than 2000 casualties. No wonder, perhaps, that Charlie only wrote: "Had about 75% casualties in the attack but were reinforced again a day or two later."

It is unfortunate though quite understandable that Charlie did not set on record more of this experience. Later, his CO, Sir Ian Hamilton, said as follows:

> May I, speaking out of a full heart, be permitted to say how gloriously the Australians and New Zealanders have upheld the finest traditions of our race during this struggle

> still in progress; at first with audacity and dash, since then with sleepless valour and untiring resource. They have already created for their countries an imperishable record of military virtue.

On 24 May there was a truce to bury the dead. Soon after this Charlie became ill. From 7 June until 8 July he was out of action with dysentery (described more modestly as "diarrhoea" on his service record) picked up in the filthy conditions of the battlefield. The minesweeper *Clacton* transferred him to the French hospital ship *Canada* and he was hospitalised in Malta on 14 June. New Zealand newspapers reported, incorrectly, that he had been wounded, though the difference was hardly relevant. The *Grey River Argus* of 26 June said:

> Private Charles Jacobsen has been wounded at the Dardanelles ... Charlie was an adept in the water and possessed a medal for lifesaving and numerous others in the way of prizes secured by him at swimming carnivals. His many exhibitions of diving in the Hokitika Municipal Bath were very interesting to the large number of people who attended to witness his performances. His many friends here will be glad to learn of his early recovery.

Indeed he did recover rapidly, and was eager to rejoin his mates even though the doctors tried to persuade him to recuperate longer. Soon he embarked on HMS *Scotian*, rejoining his unit at Gallipoli on 8 July.

Hospital ship *Canada*, April 1915

Charlie returned to duty at Gallipoli via the *SS Scotian*, but was wounded soon after arriving.

However, on 7 August, the first day of the battle for Chunk Bair, Charlie sustained a second wound. The record of this is unclear and contradictory: his service record describes it as a gunshot wound to the ankle while a contemporary newspaper report called it a shrapnel wound to the shoulder. Charlie's own record makes no reference to any shrapnel, and he even recorded a different date, 9 August. Perhaps it was two wounds but he made light of the shrapnel.

The incident was described in a letter home by one of his mates, Private W. Reid, of Greymouth:

> On August 7th our company came under heavy shrapnel fire from the Turkish 75 guns. For two hours we lay on the side of a hill, on which the shells burst with unerring accuracy. Our mates were going, two and three at a time. Our sergeant-major received a fragment of shell through his hat from the first sally, and took it off to show us what a narrow escape he had; the very next shell practically blew his head away. Two men and myself squeezed into a shallow excavation, about six inches [15 cm] deep. I was the centre one of the three, and we survived eight or nine shells O.K., but the tenth burst just a little in front of our miserable shelter and killed the man on the left side of me, whilst it inflicted a nasty wound on the leg of my other comrade. How I escaped is more than I can understand. We must have had quite two-thirds of our company put out of action in that short space of time. Major Cribb, Major Houlker, Captain Jervois, Lieutenant Duncan, Sergeants G. Hogben, L. G. Wylde and Baker, and Privates Donaldson and Charles Jacobsen were all wounded here ...

Sub-lieutenant Charles Jacobsen RN. A portrait from later in World War 1 when he served in the navy after having been an infantryman – a most unusual military career.

Next day saw some of the greatest heroism of the war when the Wellington Battalion captured the hill of Chunuk Bair and for the first and only time in the campaign Allied troops could see their original objective, the Dardanelles. However, soon they were driven off by massive Turkish counter-attacks and suffered terrible losses.

Soon Charlie was aboard the SS *Esmeraldo* lying offshore out of range of the Turkish heavy artillery, awaiting evacuation to hospital in Egypt. In retrospect it was a stroke of fortune to receive a light wound, though no soldier would have looked at it that way at the time.

In a letter to his mother Charlie described what had happened:

> The day after I landed back in the trenches I got dysentery again, but managed to hang out until I got hit in the ankle on August 9th. I was then sent to Heliopolis Hospital in Cairo, when my foot healed up all right. I am in the transport now at Alexandria. We don't have much walking to do here, but have plenty of riding and driving. So it does not affect my foot at all. I have still got dysentery —have had it off and on now for over four months. I don't think that I will ever get rid of it while I am in Egypt.
> People in New Zealand have no idea what war is like. I was in the landing on the Peninsula on April 25th, and came away on August 10th, 15 weeks altogether, and was away with dysentery a little over three weeks out of that time. So you can see that I had a little fighting. I belong to the Scouts, and was sharp-shooting the whole time I was there."

This time he was out of action for almost five months. His discharge from hospital in Alexandria was reported in New Zealand in the *Evening Post* of 11 December, but he did not rejoin his battalion at Ismailia until the 30th, by which time the Gallipoli campaign was over. Charlie also missed the battle of Kaiajik Aghala in late August and the great November snowstorm.

Of the 8556 New Zealanders who served on Gallipoli, 2721 died and 4752 were wounded, a casualty rate of six out of seven. The whole Gallipoli experience was highly traumatic for all involved and it is obvious that Charlie saw his share of the action and more. Tellingly, he remarked that he had never smoked more than a couple of packets of cigarettes in his life before Gallipoli, but afterwards he never stopped.

Still the war was far from over for Charlie, however: "After we evacuated Gallipoli we went to France, then our first big battle was on the 1st Somme when we were advancing against the Germans …"

He was in the newly established New Zealand Division, including three infantry brigades, which left Egypt for France, arriving on 6 April 1916. It concentrated in the northern part of the country west of Armentieres for brief final training before joining 50 other British and allied divisions on the Western Front to take part in the first Battle of the Somme.

Charlie wrote little about this experience except to record where he went: Abbeville, then Armentieres, then the Somme.

> One of my friends, Harold Emms, was with me in the War, attached to the Royal Engineers, during the 1st Somme (1916). When we were advancing, the Germans were firing a lot of shells, which we thought were duds because they didn't explode. All we could smell was tear gas, which has quite a nice smell but makes your eyes water. Harold Emms came running back and told us to put on our gas masks, that the Germans were also was firing up phosgene and chlorine gas, then he sort of fell down, overcome by the gas. Some of the boys ran back and told the Colonel and everybody put on their masks, which saved the rest of them. That was the last I saw of Harold until I came home from the war in 1919.

Emms died not long after the war, largely from the effects of being gassed.

Still the war was not over for Charlie. With his seafaring experience and a need for more men to staff the ships running the naval blockade of Germany, in 1917 the allied powers found yet another new role for him – this time as a naval officer, with the rank of Engineering Sub-lieutenant. This would have been quite a step up for a man who had previously been a private in the army.

The naval war is often regarded as a sideshow in World War 1 but in fact it was a critical part, especially the blockade. Since the declaration of war in August 1914 German food production could not keep up with demand and the Royal Navy intercepted all cargo vessels bound for Germany. They laid minefields to sink German ships and prevent neutral countries from trading with Germany. The blockade crippled the German economy and starvation loomed. Without surface warships to challenge the Royal Navy, the Germans felt forced into unrestricted submarine warfare, which soon began to take its toll, sinking nearly two million tonnes of shipping in the first three months. Britain began to doubt her ability to win the war if this continued.

The first ship Charlie joined was an armed merchant cruiser of the 10th Cruiser Squadron, a group of more than 40 converted merchant ships helping to enforce the blockade. These ships were highly vulnerable and about a quarter of them were lost, including the New Zealand ship *Aotearoa* (renamed *Avenger*), which had been requisitioned at the outbreak of war. Gradually however the combination of convoys and greater success at sinking submarines turned the tide again.

The ships Charlie served on operated on the North Sea from Scapa Flow to Iceland and Greenland. They did 42 days at a time at sea, followed by 10 days in port during which as many men as possible would go on leave.

The night after they sailed on Charlie's first trip, from Glasgow, he was introduced to the fleet commander and played bridge with him and some other officers. The commander quizzed him about his experiences at Gallipoli and told him he had been commander of the destroyer flotilla that supported the landing. This immediately gave them some common ground and the commander asked Charlie to shake hands with him.

Charlie recorded that the blockade was very monotonous:

> You did not know where you would be next, only that you would usually relieve the next ship that was due for a refit. Sometime you would be close to Scotland, next time over near Greenland. We used to get a bit of excitement at times when some of the ships refused to pull up when signalled. But it was more exciting when a German raider got out and two of us went after her. We chased her up to Spitzbergen but she got away from us. Another of our cruisers caught up with her but it was hard luck for her as she had only six-inch guns and the Germans had nine-inch guns and two torpedo tubes. Before he was sunk he wirelessed to another ship of ours. They sent a light cruiser out and she put an end to the raider. It was very lucky for us that we did not catch up with her as we had only 7-inch guns.

After the tide turned again against Germany on the high seas, the 10th Cruiser Squadron was no longer needed and was paid off in December 1917. Charlie was sent to Scapa Flow to join HMS *Perthshire*, feeling excited about having a

HMS *Perthshire* before her conversion to a dummy warship or "mock turtle". These defenseless ships were designed to draw fire away from the more important, real warships.

proper warship to serve on at last. But a shock awaited him when he arrived:

> The new officers all got on board a little steamer which set off to deliver each man to his ship. As each officer left, he shook hands with me and said, "Good shooting." I said, "Thanks, the same to you." Well, I was the last officer to be put off and had a yarn with the captain of the small steamer, who had been out to New Zealand several times. My turn came at last. He said, "There's your ship." I looked at her 15-inch guns, tripod mast, searchlights, anti-aircraft guns, and thought, "What a ship!" The Captain shook hands with me and said, "Good shooting and good luck." Well, you can just imagine, with everybody saying, "Good shooting," I thought what a wonderful ship I must be joining.
>
> The ship's pinnace came alongside the steamer. I collected my gear, got on board and as I stepped off the gangway I saw that all the armaments were made from wood. There were wooden guns, wooden funnels, anti-aircraft guns, searchlight, all wood. We could not have shot a sparrow.
>
> I saluted the man on the gangway and asked for the officer of the day. When he came along he asked me what I thought of the ship. I told him that I did not know she was a merchant ship until I stepped on board, which pleased him very much. He took me along to meet the Commander, who was having a game of billiards, and he too was very pleased when I told him you could not pick that she was a dummy until you stepped on deck.

Perthshire was a copy of HMS *Vanguard*, Britain's seventh dreadnought-type battleship that saw service in the Battle of Jutland and remained unscathed until an accidental explosion sank her in Scapa Flow in 1917. *Perthshire* was one of 14 dummy capital ships built to trick enemy spies and reconnaissance. The dummy warships were known as the suicide squadron, the grey armada, or the mock turtles, for they were defenseless and designed to draw fire away from the warships they mimicked. They were simply built from large antiquated merchant ships of around 9,000 tonnes.

As a British officer described it at the end of the war:

> No such colossal war jest had been played on an enemy since the days of the Trojan Empire. The British Admiralty tantalised the German navy with mysterious manoeuvres of a wooden squadron, some of the vessels made of barn lumber, and the Germans were completely baffled for months by the unexpected number of their enemies ... On board the joke was evident at once. The fighting turrets were little wooden barns, with bare rafters inside. The great guns were logs graduated from a sapling and bored in exact imitation of naval cannon ... the deck was covered with tightly stretched canvas, painted grey to represent the smooth steel deck of a man-of-war, so that reconnoitring aeroplanes would be deceived.

After that he was put on convoy work. The first trip was to Dakar on the west coast of Africa, escorting eight ships loaded with sugar for Portsmouth.

He was torpedoed twice – once while assistant engineer on the 6103-tonne merchant cruiser *Patia* and once on the *Seritor.* The ship was accompanying an American troop convoy from half way across the Atlantic from America, when about 1320 miles off the coast of Ireland she was torpedoed and sank in about 11 minutes.

After rescue he landed at Portsmouth where he got a new outfit of clothes and had about 10 days' leave. After that he was on several diesel-powered ships and stayed on them until the war finished.

He had two and a half months' leave in England before coming back to New Zealand. His uncle in Birmingham had a big Napier car and plenty of money but could not get petrol, so Charlie wrote to the Controller of Benzine for England explaining where he had been during the war, who he was staying with and the car he had. He received back a letter enclosing a big book of petrol coupons, and saying if any more New Zealanders or Aussies had been in different places

Armistice Day in Cathedral Square.

fighting he was only too pleased to give them coupons as the war was finished and restrictions were no longer so severe.

Eventually Charlie sailed home in the *Tahiti* with other New Zealand troops, arriving in July 1919. On arrival he went down to Hokitika to a wonderful reception, reported in the *Grey River Argus* of 26 July:

> PERSONAL
> One of the most interesting men among the many who have returned to the Dominion after going through wonderful exploits at the war in defense of their country is Engineer sub-Lieutenant C. E. Jacobsen, of the Royal Navy, who passed through Greymouth yesterday on his way to Hokitika, where he is to be accorded a special welcome home. He was met here yesterday by His Worship the Mayor, Captain Colclough and other gentlemen, and gave a truly fascinating account of life as it has been lived by the boys in blue on the high seas in the perilous times of armed hostilities... the Lieutenant lately came home through Nelson. He went away with the Main Body. Enlisting at Hokitika, (where he formerly used to be engineer on the well-known steamer "Jane Douglas") he first served in Egypt and Gallipoli, and then in France, being twice wounded. He was transferred to the Navy in April, 1917, and has since served on five different ships .... He says it was intensely funny to be on the "dummy" dreadnoughts. These he explains, were "armed to the teeth" with no fewer than fourteen "formidable" six-inch guns. "They could not shoot a swallow" he says, "as they were dummies like everything else about the ships." The "dummies" all lined up in their appointed places when naval operations were afoot, and the

> enemy were mightily respectful of them, and took no "risks" from them. Lieut. Jacobsen's "dreadnought," the Perthshire, on one occasion was in a tight fix, and was faced by German warships, but she brazened it out, and got through "without firing a shot." Those who have heard of his exploits are satisfied that Lieut. Jacobsen and his comrades extracted a good deal of fun from the war.

Charlie concluded his brief reminiscences of the war by saying, "I stayed a week and then went up to Nelson, started to dig the garden for my brother Walter, who had been smacked in the back with a piece of shell in 1916."

He never talked much about the war with his descendants, though they were fascinated by the Luger pistol he had souvenired and brought home (page 95). Ian Dann recalls when he was about 9 years old,

> Granddad was sitting in his usual chair in the dining room cleaning the Luger, which just a gun to me at the time. I asked him where he got it from; he just looked up at me and said it was either him or me! At the time I didn't place too much importance on what he had just said. It was only when I got around to talking to Mum about it that I realized the gravity of the situation. I had simply taken it to mean than he fought the other soldier to get the gun!

Citation given to Charlie for his contribution to the war effort.

CHAPTER 10

Coastal seafaring days

While in Nelson Charlie saw an advertisement in the paper. Richardson & Co., Napier, wanted a man that had experience with diesel and semi-diesel engines. He got the job and started working for them almost right away.

Scows tied up in Nelson towards the end of their sailing days.

On 8 October 1919 the ship ran ashore while he was an engineer on the *Echo* carting frozen meat from Wairoa to Napier. (There was no road connecting these two Hawke's Bay towns in those days.) They used to load meat while at anchor in the Wairoa River mouth and carry a few passengers on daylight sailings. On that day there were five passengers as well as the hold full of beef. The crew could see by the amount of break on the bar that it would be almost impossible to push their way out against it, but the signal was up to take the bar so they had a try.

> I went down below and stood by the engines while the captain asked for extra revs and I gave both engines all they had. The first sea hit forward and carried away 16 feet [5 metres] of bulwark; the next rolled along the deck, right over the engine room skylight; and the third and fourth turned her sideways on. We only just cleared the outer mole, then the ship went sideways up on to the beach.
>
> The Captain rang 'finished with engines', so I closed down, wrote up the log and went up on deck. Then went down to my cabin, which was occupied by a schoolteacher. She remarked on what a rough trip we seemed to be having!
>
> I asked her if she had ever been shipwrecked and she said she hadn't. "Well," I replied, " you are now; but you can walk ashore on the starboard side without getting wet feet."
>
> The other ships nearby sent some anchors back to us to help hold the ship from being driven further up the beach. We unloaded the meat onto a truck and loaded it onto other ships the next day. Then we tried to get her off. We put the anchors well out to sea with a very heavy hawser on and brought the hawser back to the after bollards. We had a fairly powerfully geared oil winch, and throttle gear block and tackle, which we used on the winch. It looked like we shouldn't have too much trouble getting her off.
>
> However, after a week we had made no progress so the captain and mate went relieving on other ships. Then there came a period of neap tides and it was harder to get her off, though there might be a chance with the next round of spring tides in two weeks' time. The crew were paid off but they left the cook and myself on board. The owners told me if I thought there was any chance to get her off to ring them up and they would send someone to give a hand. Otherwise, sooner or later I suppose there would have been a storm or heavy swells and she would have been a wreck.
>
> Soon enough the next spring tides came and piled sand and shingle all around her and put a lot on deck as well. The cook and I shovelled it all off the deck and had to wait again for a fortnight. When the tides started to get a little near the spring tide I could see that this time the sea was going to wash the ship clear. All the sand was washed away by the second to

Charlie all dressed up in his glad rags.

Mary Jacques with her brother Mervyn.

highest tide, and things were becoming clear underneath the ship. I got all the mooring tackle ready, then that night got the engines ready to start. This time the waves did not roll right over her, but loosened a lot of shingle under the stern. So the next day, just before the highest tide she started to move a little. I got the winch going and took up the tension very tightly on the anchor, then set both engines going astern. The prop wash kicked the rest of the sand and gravel clear and we gave another very hard pull and she came off. I shifted some of the weight from aft to for'ard, left the engines running out of gear, tied an empty oil drum to the hawser and cast it off. Then I steered the *Echo* into the breastwork inside the harbour, where the cook hopped ashore to take the lines while I kept her alongside. I went up to the agent, told him that the ship was off the beach and was ready to be taken to Napier as soon as they could get the crew together. We left the next morning for Napier, where we went on the slip and discovered that even after a month aground the only damage was that all the copper paint had been scrubbed off by the shingle.

One day he earned the easiest £10 he made in a long time, and also saved the ship's owners an expensive bill for a diver to clear a rope tangled around the propellor:

It happened after we were going alongside the wharf and somehow one of the mooring ropes got foul of the starboard propeller. It soon became wound tightly around it and I could go neither ahead nor astern. The rope was about 3½ inches [87 mm] in diameter so I had to tell the captain that the starboard engine was out of action and explain what was the matter with it. He went ashore after the ship was made fast and the agent came back with him. He wanted the ship to sail that night but the captain would not take her out on just one engine. It would take a day to get a diver from Napier and cost about £20 for a taxi, plus the diver's expenses would be another £15. I said, "Give me £10 and I'll get it free in half an hour. They jumped at this, so I said, "Just put that in writing and you can see me do it." They signed a bill so I got a very sharp knife, tied it to my waist, went over the stern, dived down, hung onto the stern bracket with one hand, and cut the rope with the knife in the other hand. It took four dives to get it all off. Easy.

> While I was still on the *Echo*, in May 1920 Richardson & Co. decided to sell her as they did not have enough cargo to keep all their fleet busy. Mr Eckford came up from Blenheim and bought her for running freight all around the southern regions. I gave him a guarantee that I would stay for twelve months.

Fred Ward was second engineer with Charlie while they were on the run carrying coal from Puponga to Picton. He introduced Charlie to his cousin Mary Jacques, whom he married in 1924. Mary was working in the bakery at Picton at that time.

The scow carted coal to Picton for over six months, then went all over the place with different cargoes. In late 1920 on a trip from Foxton to Wellington with a load of flax fibre, the crankshaft broke on the starboard engine. They managed to limp into Wellington then across to Blenheim where Charlie dismantled the engine and took the crankshaft out ready to put a new one in.

Christmas passed and Charlie was still on holiday and away in Greymouth when one day Mr Eckford rang him up and asked him to relieve the engineer on his other ship, the *Omaka*. He went up to Blenheim and Mr Eckford told him to take his tools and gear aboard and she would sail after dinner. He had just done so when Eckford changed his mind and told him to take his gear ashore and go by the *Wairau* the

Mary posing on the river bank.

Mary and Charlie's wedding day, 1924. From left to right: Mervyn Jacques, Charles Jacobsen, Mary Jacobsen and Myrtle Briscoe.

Mary as a baby.

next day to take the *Echo* crankshaft to Stephens & Cook in Port Chalmers. Off he went, taking the shaft by the *Wahine* to Lyttelton, then by train to Port Chalmers. When he got up the next morning and went to the smoking room of the hotel, someone told him there had been a terrible shipwreck in Wellington. A small ship had been lost with all hands. It was the *Omaka*! And Charlie hadn't even told his wife about the change of plan. She thought he'd been aboard the lost ship when he was in fact safe and sound in Dunedin. This was just one of many scares Charlie gave poor old Mary over the years.

The *Omaka* wreck was caused by sudden capsize in a squall at the harbour entrance. A lighthouse keeper witnessed the dying struggles of the six crew, who clung to the wreckage and tragically missed being spotted by a steamer that passed close by. It is interesting to speculate whether Charlie, with his great physical strength and swimming skills, might have survived this event and used up yet another of his nine lives. This was, after all, not the first time he had cheated death in the treacherous waters around Cook Strait; and nor would it be the last.

After the *Echo* was repaired and back in service, Charlie only stayed with her for another six months before he became ill. He went to a doctor in Wellington, who recognised there was some kind of respiratory problem and asked if he'd been gassed in the war. Charlie said he had, a little, but also mentioned that the smokestack on the *Echo* came out of the stern, and with a following wind would fill the cabin up with exhaust gas. The doctor said, "You're still getting gassed where you are. If you want to live, go bush felling or get some other job out in the open."

So Charlie swallowed the anchor ... for a while. He went bushfelling for six months, but soon went to sea again, this time down the west coast as engineer on a small ship running a service to South Westland. After he left, he noted that they fixed the exhaust on the *Echo* ... too late for him.

The little vessel he joined was running mail and cargo to Okarito, Bruce Bay, Okuru and Jackson Bay. "It was quite a nice little run in fine weather but from Greymouth to Jackson Bay there was no shelter anywhere and more often it was a rough trip."

After about six months the west coast farmers bought their own little ship, so Charlie went trawling out of Greymouth for a while, then worked as a fitter in the Greymouth railway workshops for about nine months. Then a big floating dredge in Hokitika needed an engineer to work on its Vickers-Petter 2-stroke diesel engines, so he applied and got the job. These engines were a new type of very large (210-litre) and powerful (200 bhp) diesel engine. By this time the chaos of the early gold rushes had settled down and many claims had become consolidated into gigantic open-cast mines. These were worked by enormous dredges floating on pontoons in a pond that moved with them as they dredged from the front end and piled up tailings at the back.

This was the first spud dredge in New Zealand. The "spuds" were two big vertical steel pipes, each about 15 tonnes, that slid up and down in tubes on either side of the barge. They would drop one spud down so it would sink into the mud and gravel at the bottom of the dredge pond. The dredge had a chain of buckets on a boom that would swing in an arc to collect all the gravel within reach, then the

Myrtle Briscoe and Mary.

Mary and Charlie off on their honeymoon.

Gold dredge on the Buller River, about 1900.

other spud would be dropped and the dredge would move ahead. The frame that held this piece of machinery went under the dredge about 6 metres, and to wind each spud up there was a gantry about 15 metres high. The operation went on night and day except from midnight on Saturday to midnight on Sunday. Many dredges like this were very profitable for their owners and worked enormous areas all the way across the coastal plains, leaving tailings heaps that are still visible today.

It was while working on this job that Charlie had what he described as the worst experience of his life. There was a very bad leak in the pontoons that could not be located from inside the dredge, and they needed to know how much damage was done underneath. A diver would have to come from Wellington to assess the damage and this would have taken over a week, plus perhaps much longer to actually make the repairs.

The manager heard that Charlie was very good at

A very different type of dredge, one that worked to keep the port of Westport open to steamers plying the coal trade around the country.

underwater swimming and asked him if he would go down under the dredge and try to locate the problem. Charlie said he would give it a go, figuring it should not be too difficult as the dredge only drew a bit over 2 metres and the farthest he would have to swim under water was about 8 metres. It didn't seem too dangerous.

He tied a very strong rope round his waist and lowered a weight so he could slide down to the bottom of the dredge. He took a powerful watertight lamp and got a chap he trusted with his life (someone who had been to the war with him) to take charge of the safety procedures (such as they were): "If I give three light pulls on the rope, haul me up steady, but if I give three sharp ones, pull me as fast as you can." The spuds were lowered back behind the dredge and Charlie told the manager to make sure they stayed that way while he was under the dredge.

> Well, down I went, got under the dredge about 4 or 5 feet [1.6 m], but couldn't even see the electric light as the water was thick with mud and it was as dark as night. I gave three light pulls and they hauled me up. I told the manager what it was like and asked him if he had a blueprint showing the bottom of the dredge so that I could see what it was supposed to be like. Then I would be able to feel my way and be able to report if anything was not as it should be.
>
> After having a good look at the blueprint I went down again. I slid down the rope with the weight tied on to it until I got to the bottom, then started to pull myself along underneath by the stay that held the spud in place. I got about 20 feet [6 m] along when I found the break, feeling along with my left hand while I kept myself in position with my right. The heavy steel frame underneath had broken. I was feeling under the broken piece so that I would be able to tell them what it was like, when without a second's warning, bang, the outside piece flattened on my wrist, jammed it hard on the bottom of the dredge and nearly crushing the bone.
>
> Just imagine how I felt, pinned there all alone in the blackness, caught like a rat in a trap. I didn't even have a knife to cut my hand off, which might have afforded some chance of escape. I said to myself, "This is where you get it, old boy. Been to the war, all through Gallipoli, torpedoed twice in the navy, very nearly killed at high diving, smashed up twice bike racing,

stabbed with a knife, wounded twice ... and all just to end up dying like this..."

By this time I had been under water over two and a half minutes. I had made up my mind that before I lost consciousness and started to breathe water, I would give the rope three pulls but knew what the result would be. The rope would have broken and they might have realised what they had done. This is what they did. Somebody took a pull on the gantry that lifted the spud. It came up and jammed me and I knew that if they did not release that rope I was finished. So I said, "This is where you test your long diving." I did not move, tried to stop my heart from racing but it started to hammer so hard I thought they would hear it on the dredge. I felt my self starting to get giddy, must be near the four minute mark, and was just going to try a mouthful of water which I knew would be 20 seconds after, I would be unconscious, got the rope in my hand, and they must have let go the pull, because I jerked loose the hand that was jammed, taking all the skin off. I yanked on the rope three pulls. That is all I remember until 15 or 20 minutes later when I came to on the dredge.

I told the manager what had happened. He took me straight to the nearest hotel. I had a hot brandy. He took me home, sent for the doctor. I was in bed three days and recovered completely, but I don't want an experience like that again.

Crossing the notoriously dangerous Hokitika river bar.

Still Charlie had one more dangerous adventure to come on the west coast before leaving the region permanently. He took work on the 30-tonne auxiliary ketch *Wakaiti*, on a journey to establish timber ownership in south Westland. The story, which has some of the elements of a Wild West adventure, was reported in the *Greymouth Star* of 22 July 1924:

"ALL IN!"

WAKAITI BEATS TASMAN.

—

STIRRING STORY OF THE SEA

Dirty, unshaven and heavy-eyed through lack of sleep, three men stepped on to the Greymouth wharf yesterday, thankful to be alive. They were all in, after a continuous fight of nearly a fortnight against the fury of the storm-tossed Tasman, in a little cockleshell of a ketch, the *Wakaiti*, of 30 tons odd. Their story possesses all the elements of a romance and, indeed, sounds more like fiction than fact.

Lying snugly at her berth in the lagoon, out of commission for the winter, the *Wakaiti* did not expect to be called upon at short notice to point her bows into the South until the next fishing season. But a race for timber was in progress between two powerful syndicates, the prize being the rights over millions of pounds worth of virgin timber in the untouched forests of South Westland. The rights were, available for disposal, and the first party on the spot reaped the fruits of victory.

Motor transit was employed by one of the syndicates and they gained a good lead upon their rivals. The latter, represented by Messrs E. Rundle and Wallis, were not going to give up the contest easily, and proceeded to charter the *Wakaiti* for the trip South. Her regular skipper, Captain Jolley, was not on deck, having accepted a position as head bushman at Ruatapu, while her A.B., Mr. "Dodger" Cronin, was unable to make the trip owing to illness among the members of his family.

A volunteer crew was quickly secured, and at 1 a.m. on July 10 the *Wakaiti* put to sea, manned by Mr. W. Reeves, signalman at Greymouth, as skipper; Mr. C. S. Jacobsen, Greymouth, as engineer; and Mr. J. Hopkins, of Greymouth, as able seaman. Messrs Rundle and Wallis were the passengers.

Steadily, driven south by her twin Skandia engines, developing 90 horse power, the *Wakaiti* was off Ross before the trouble commenced to come along her way. Then bad fuel resulted in engine failure, the pipes becoming blocked. Mr. Jacobsen effected repairs, but shortly afterwards a second blockage occurred, and finally the pipes burst.

The ketch was then opposite the Little Wanganui River [actually the Wanganui River near Harihari] and the engineer was continuously occupied all the way to Jackson's Bay in repairing the pipes in first one and then the other engine. He now confesses to wishing for a sample of his impromptu repair work as a souvenir of his most eventful trip. The troubles of those on board were increased by the advent of a "howling nor-wester," and about 80 miles north of Jackson's Bay the exhaust pipe was stove in by the heavy seas and the *Wakaiti* began to leak. Then commenced a grim battle with the water; the pumps could not handle the inflow, and the water in the vessel gradually rose to a depth of four feet, and the prospects of reaching port in safety looked blue. They battled on, however, and managed to reach Jackson's Bay, described by Mr. Jacobsen as "the best anchorage north of Milford Sound," on Saturday, July 12, just before noon. The storm still raged, and that night the *Wakaiti* dragged two anchors and 40 fathoms of cable, the weary crew having to man the engines and head out to sea.

They spent a miserable night, great seas continually breaking over the little vessel. About 11 a.m. on the following day, Sunday, the weather moderated, enabling repairs to be effected and the ketch pumped dry.

Unable to get near enough to the shore to land the passengers, and the ketch not carrying a dinghy, another problem presented itself. It was solved by the plucky skipper and engineer, who swam a quarter of a mile to the shore through ice-cold water, known to be infested with sharks. They landed, in safety and succeeded in launching a boat. Messrs Bundle and Wallis were put ashore, and set off on a nine-mile walk to secure horses, on which they completed the remainder of the journey of about 20 miles to Okuru, their destination.

Preparations for the return to Greymouth were then made by the *Wakaiti's* crew, and they managed to secure two cases of fuel at Jackson's Bay. The two leaks in the vessel were plugged; the engine pipes repaired, and the ketch pumped out, all hands doing their share of the work. Weather conditions were still dead against them, and it was necessary to shelter in Jackson's Bay for four days.

The Tasman finally relented temporarily, and the *Wakaiti* left Jackson's Bay astern at nine o'clock last Friday night. There was no wind and the weather was beautiful. Not for long, however. The ketch had proceeded only as far as Okarito when Old Man Tasman again let loose his fury, and a terrific sou'-wester came up about midday. Engine trouble again developed and one engine stopped. A jury sail was rigged from an old cattle cover, and the skipper headed away from the shore.

The force of the gale was too much for the sail, and less than half an hour after it was rigged the canvas and rigging, was torn away and disappeared in the raging sea. The engineer had not been idle meanwhile, and by strenuous efforts succeeded in again repairing the engine.

By 8 o'clock on Saturday night the rudder carried away and the ketch was practically at the mercy of the towering waves, estimated to be 40 feet high. It became necessary to heave to for the night, and all hands faced the task of rigging a sea anchor. This was achieved by the use of a spar, four barrels, 60 fathoms of chain and 80 fathoms of wire rope. All through the wild night the waves dashed over the helpless *Wakaiti*, but she came through the ordeal splendidly.

On Sunday morning the voyage was resumed, and it says much for the seamanship of the skipper and his crew that the ketch was steered from a point about 18 miles south of Ross by manoeuvring her engines, working first one and then the other. To the fact that the vessel has twin engines, making such an expedient possible, Mr. Jacobsen ascribes the saving of the vessel and the lives of those on board her.

Greymouth roadstead was a welcome sight when it was reached at 11.30 a.m. on Sunday, and the mariners signalled for the assistance of the tug. Disappointment again awaited them, as the sea on the bar was too rough to permit the tug to cross. The ketch was headed about four miles out to sea, and by dint of running the engines alternately, she was kept moving in a circle.

The adventurers were not content idly to wait for the tug, however, and made shift to help themselves by attempting to rig a temporary rudder.

The skipper and engineer again took to the water, diving overboard and endeavouring to carry out the job. The icy water and rough sea, combined with the pitching and tossing of the vessel, defeated them, and they resumed their wait for the tug. The vigil ended about noon yesterday, and the *Wakaiti* was towed in, with a barrel on the wire rope astern to keep her head on to the sea. Onlookers considered that the ketch had a rough trip crossing the bar, but Mr. Jacobsen says that it was only a tenth of the sea encountered down South.

Talking to a "Star" reporter, he said that he had been connected with the *Wakaiti* since she was built by Mr. Park at Hokitika in 1913, but had never seen such a heavy sea. He left Hokitika in 1914 for 'the front as a member of the Main Body and was slightly gassed at the Somme. He then joined the Navy, holding the rank of Engineer-Lieutenant for two and a half years." The *Wakaiti* is a marvellous boat," he said, "and will ride over any waves as long as she is tight."

He remarked that when at Jackson's Bay he was so exhausted that sleep became essential and he dropped off for two hours in the forecastle. When he awoke there was water 4ft. deep in the vessel.

He was glad to be able to allay his wife's anxiety regarding the fate of the *Wakaiti*, and sent a message by Messrs Rundle and Wallis for transmission to Greymouth when they reached the first means of communication. He paid a tribute to the seamanship of Mr. Reeves, and said that his conduct on the *Wakaiti* was another example of the bravery displayed by him on the occasion of the Reefton picnic tragedy on the Greymouth beach, when he risked his life to rescue others. Mr. Hopkins also praised the skill of the skipper. "He is a real seaman," was his verdict ...The skill, grit and determination shown by the men who brought the *Wakaiti* to port through the howling gales of the Tasman will not soon be forgotten by the men of the waterfront, in whose welcome to the returned adventurers yesterday there was nothing lacking.

CHAPTER 11

Early days at French Pass

By this time Charlie and Mary had two children, Mary (known as Molly, born 1924) and Charles (1927, who was always known as "Young Charlie"). While his family continued to live in Greymouth, Charlie got a job on a trawler bound for Nelson and after last being heard from in Wanganui he disappeared for a couple of years. All he ever recorded of this period was: "Went up to Wanganui, had a lot of bad luck. Came back to the French Pass and started fishing there." This part of his life is a real mystery as nobody knows where he was and what he got up to.

Poor Mary had no money and there was no government support or family benefit in those days. She had to make the children's clothes out of flour and sugar sacks and depended on the charity of friends and neighbours to keep the family fed. In later years, after Charlie reappeared on the scene, there were rumours of an illegitimate child by a Maori mother, and many other things that could be true and might just as well not be.

We next catch up with him in the Sounds, where he started fishing for himself. He rented a house in Katherine Cove on D'Urville Island, about 10 km north of French Pass, then made contact with Mary again and moved her and the two children there from Greymouth with all their worldly goods. You may wonder why she took him back, but what choice did she have? Then, within two months after getting back with Charlie she was pregnant with their third child. The year was 1929 and he took Mary up to Picton to have

My mother, Noeline Jacobsen.

the baby, a girl they called Noeline – my mother, whose story you can read in much more detail in my first book *Horncastle's Suitcase*.

Charlie managed to scrape up a small deposit and a took out a loan to buy a 32-foot (9 metre) flush-deck launch called the *Peerless* (built in 1912 by Bailey and Lowe, a well-known Auckland boat builder). The *Peerless* had a 25 hp Sterling petrol motor and a good cabin as it had been a passenger ferry before Charlie got it. It was very low in the water so the name was a bit ironic. He went handlining and longlining for blue cod and groper at French Pass. It's a bit of a mystery where he got the money as his father would only lend him money to buy a farm. It was right in the middle of the depression and people were extremely cautious (not to mention poverty-stricken). Farmers only understood farming and they certainly couldn't relate to the idea of operating a launch for a living. But Old Charlie took to it like a duck to water and soon became a bit of a legend in the Sounds.

Charlie also thought about the freight and mail run he

Looking through the narrow tidal race of French Pass, from the south (Tasman Bay) end to the north (Cook Strait) end. D'Urville Island is on the left, the South Island on the right. In the background, Katherine Cove, where the Jacobsens first lived in the Sounds, lies tucked inside the long peninsula.

French Pass in the 1930s.

worked on down the west coast and it gave him the idea to start up one in the French Pass area. He began with a weekly run into Port Hardy, then into Greville Harbour. There was enough demand for the service though the money was poor as the great depression was in full swing, so he could barely earn enough to put food on the table. They virtually lived on fish and what they could grow in the garden, and if he hadn't been able to do his own repairs on the boat they would have gone bankrupt. Mary was still making the children's clothes out of flour and sugar bags, and all their clothes had patches everywhere but it was the same for most people at the time.

Eventually the price of fish improved and they were also able to charge more for freight. Then Charlie put a new 20 hp diesel engine in the *Peerless*. Everybody said that it would be no good but they didn't have his experience and know-how. Charlie could see that diesel was the way of the future for marine engines.

Charlie pulling in groper on a long-line.

Charlie had a very close shave one day when he nearly wrecked the boat. He had two crew working for him at the time and they were coming back to French Pass one day in a hurry to catch the steamer. They were flat out gutting two sacks of blue cod to have them ready in time, while also trying to grab a bite of lunch. As a result they got distracted and ran the launch into a rock, tearing about 1.5 metres of plank on the starboard side below the water line. Charlie yelled out to one of the men to sit in the hole to try and stem the rush of water, which he did. Then he told the other one to get a buoy on a long rope and tied one end to the boat so if she sank they would know where to locate her. They had about four miles to go to the shore and they managed to beach her just as the water became almost level with the engine air intake. Charlie then sent one man to walk 8 km over the hill to where another chap had a launch, telling him to bring back a saw, hammer and nails.

The Nelson to Wellington ferry MV *Matai* going through French Pass with the ebbing tide.

Meanwhile Charlie realised the tide had just started to ebb when they hit the shore, so soon the hull would be high and dry. The *Peerless* had stranded on her damaged side so they had to scrape away the rocks and stones underneath to get at the hole. Charlie always carried a small piece of canvas and they nailed that over the hole. Then they tied a rope to a rock near low tide mark and waited for the launch, which arrived in good time to get them off on the next high tide. Charlie had managed to make the basic repair all by himself but still got the launch to escort them home. The *Peerless* never made a bucket of water in the 25 miles of steaming, so they got home all right but lost all the fish, all their gear, and were cold and wet through.

French Pass light, marking the rocks.

They hauled the launch up on the slip and put in some new planks. The vessel was no worse off for the experience, the engine never had any problem and ran well for many years afterwards.

In 1931 a small steamer going through French Pass had hit the middle beacon and turned abeam to it, with the full force of the tide holding her there. This cracked the foundations and put a lean on the light. The lighthouse expert from the Marine Department decided to put a metre of foundations all around the beacon to strengthen it and got Charlie to do the launch work. The might of the tidal flow made it quite an exciting job, although Charlie's claim that it reached 18 knots is an exaggeration,. But even at 8 knots it was still about the most fierce current anywhere around the coast of New Zealand.

First they fitted a cylinder about 60 cm high all around the base and poured quick-drying cement into it. They could only do this at low tide and it took quite a while to get it level. They also had to chip the rock away so it would fit. Then they made a canvas sleeve to go right around the beacon while all the cement was mixed on the beach and carried out in a dinghy – 750 kg at a time, all in buckets. Charlie would tow the dinghy behind the *Peerless,* then a helper would jump on the beacon, haul the dinghy alongside and hand up the buckets of cement to be poured into the cylinder. As the tide began to rise they would lower the canvas cover until it was all round so that the tide would not wash the cement away before it could set. It was a tricky job. Sometimes the tide would not go down low enough for them to work.

Other times as soon as they got started the wind would blow and put up a sea and they would have to stop or be washed off. It took them about three months to do the job and the beacon is still standing today. Charlie said he wouldn't have missed the experience for anything, though they did have a close shave one day when their mooring rope broke. The launch drifted straight into a dangerous patch of water known as Jacob's Whirlpool, where the flow passes over shallow rocks then drops into deep water. For a while the launch just drifted round and round in circles. There was a young chap on board who had been working for Charlie about a month and supposedly knew how to start the engine and drive the boat, but when Charlie called out instructions to him he got too excited and forgot to put his foot on the

Some of the Jacobsen children, about 1936. Left to right: Young Charlie, Molly, Noeline, Jean and Phyllis.

decompression lever, so he couldn't get the engine to start. Charlie had to row across to him in the dinghy, and as the launch got to the edge of the whirlpool he jumped on board, tied the dinghy to the back, started the engine and steamed up to the beacon again. After that the young chap had had enough of the adventurous life at French Pass and Charlie had to put him on the steamer to go home that night.

Even while Charlie was having all these adventures he must have spent some time at home because Mary was continuing to have babies every year or so. Noeline was closely followed by Phyllis (1931), Jean (1933), Eric (1935), Zilla (1939), and finally David in 1942. Each time he would have to take Mary to Picton to stay with her parents while she had the baby. Of course, whenever Charlie hit town he would carry on his drinking and hell-raising ways, and this caused bad feeling among his Irish in-laws who were concerned about their daughter being stuck with this wild man and not having the life they had hoped for her.

Every few months Charlie seemed to have yet another life-threatening experience. One day he was going in to Port Hardy at the northwestern end of D'Urville Island, where the tidal flow can be very strong. He had two passengers on board, a Mr and Mrs Flaghorn. They were just going in to Port Hardy when the tide began to ebb and a westerly wind came up. Wind against current always creates a dangerous, confused sea but if they had gone straight in they might have been all right. However, the seas made Mrs Flaghorn nervous and she insisted on going back to the sheltered side

Another family gathering. From left: Eric, Jean, Keith Dann, Phyllis, Noeline, Charlie, Kathleen Aston, Rita Jacobsen (cousin), Myrtle, Zilla, David and Old Mary.

of the island, a distance of ten miles, then walking over the hill to Port Hardy instead. By the time Charlie had done this and was on his way back to Port Hardy with only his deckhand on board, the ebbing tidal current was flowing full bore and the wind had increased to 30 knots. Charlie had to steer his way through some rocks called the Sixties and just as he turned the corner a sea picked the launch up and shot her ahead like a rocket. He was steering from on deck as this gave him better control of the rudder and could move the tiller more quickly. He told the deckhand to close the throttle but the guy didn't respond quickly enough so the launch buried itself in a big green one right up to the wheelhouse. Then before it could shake the water off another wave broke right on to the cockpit, filling her up with about 60 cm of water. Charlie managed to close the throttle and bring the launch's head around on to the next one but it took them two hours to pump the water out.

After that he anchored off the Flaghorns' home, where they gave him a change of clothes and he stayed for the night. As soon as they got back to French Pass he had three hatches made for the *Peerless*, and always carried them afterwards. It used to take about five minutes to put them in place when the weather turned threatening and probably saved them from many other near-catastrophes. As Charlie said later, "If we had taken another one that day it would have been the finish of us. With the tide and the heavy sea we would not have been able to swim out of it as the shore was sheer cliffs."

By this time the launch service had become established and was ending the total isolation of the Sounds way of life. Charlie had all the mail and freight for the whole area, including D'Urville and Stevens Islands. In fact the *Peerless* was too small for the task and couldn't handle the weather. It was totally the wrong sort of boat for the job, but the Jacobsens couldn't do anything about it. They had no money. The world was in the depths of the greatest depression ever, so other people didn't have much to spend on his services either. Fishing was an essential supplement to their income and food supplies, and Charlie had to use all his seamanship skills and work around the weather.

The Jacobsen house at Fennel Bay (today known as Waikawa Bay), before the great slip that destroyed it. This location, on the mainland just a few km southwest of French Pass, was ideal for Charlie's launch operation.

By the time his son Young Charlie was aged 8 he had started working on the boat, so he got very little education and went through his life unable to read or write, although this never stopped him from succeeding in business.

With an ever-expanding family Charlie had to find a bigger house and a better situation for his growing mail and fishing business. So they bought a six-roomed house in Fennel Bay, which had a good mooring for the launch and was closer to French Pass for meeting up with the steamers that passed through between Wellington or Picton and Nelson. They used to rendezvous at 10 pm (northbound) and 3 am (southbound) for transshipping mail and freight as the steamer slowed down going through French Pass. I will expand on the ferry story later.

As a child I remember my mother talking about scallops lying in the shallow water of Fennel Bay, and crayfish being plentiful and easy to catch although they never ate them. Mary spent a lot of time baking to feed a growng family, and clothes were patched and handed down as each child grew out of each garment. The depression was still in full swing

MV *Noeline* moored in Fennel Bay.

and they ate a lot of fish, grew vegetables and fruit, swapped fish for sheep from the farmers, and had a house cow that the children had to milk every day. There was very little money for groceries that they only got once a month They kept hens and kept the surplus eggs in earthenware containers in a solution of waterglass to preserve them.

There was no money for toys but my aunties told me if the wind was blowing off the land they would make boats out of flaxwood (the very light woody branches on which flax flowers are borne) with a bird's feather for a sail and a shell for a keel, and see whose would go fastest. Sometimes when Charlie was coming home from around D'Urville Island he would see their little boats sailing far out at sea.

The house was lit with kerosene lamps and the heating was from an old wood-burning stove and an open fireplace. Having been a blacksmith-cum-engineer Charlie decided to dam the stream behind the house and make a small hydro power generation system. He piped the water from a dam through a small nozzle on to a Pelton wheel with a generator connected with belts and wiring running back to the house. It took him a couple of months to build and the family was excited about having lights just like in town. But Charlie couldn't get it to go. I suspect there was not enough head of water, which wouldn't have delivered enough pressure to drive the wheel. Charlie was not one to give up quickly so he kept changing things to try and make it work. But one day his foul temper got the better of him and smashed it to bits with a sledgehammer. After that the family never spoke about it again.

Fennel Bay 2014
(now called Camp Bay).

CHAPTER 12

The gamble to build the *Noeline*, 1933

Charlie knew he needed to be able to offer a reliable and regular service so he could retain the mail contract whenever it came up for renewal. So he did his circuit every Friday regardless of the weather (which is ironic because seafarers consider it bad luck to sail on a Friday). This meant a lot of trips that were very unpleasant, plus heavy wear and tear on the launch although he could carry out most of the repairs himself.

My grandfather was very good at staying alive, but knew it was a numbers game and sooner or later his name would come up if he keep battling the sea in a small launch. He went around to visit Claude Wells at his boatbuilding yard at Wakatahuri. The Wellses were an old Sounds family, famous for boatbuilding and wrecking old ships for materials. Literally Charlie scratched out a sketch in the dirt to show exactly what he wanted. This boat was well ahead of its time, not the normal round bottom that made boats roll in a sea but roll back easily too so they were safe and seaworthy. Charlie wanted to carry heavy loads and needed speed, even if it came at the cost of some seaworthiness. He needed deck room for fishing and a large cabin for passengers and to keep his mail and freight dry.

Claude Wells quoted him about £300 and they struck a deal. Charlie got about £200 for the *Peerless* and the buyer even advanced the money before taking delivery of the boat so Charlie could continue the mail run until the new vessel was complete. He put up about £150 as a deposit. Claude

How the *Noeline* looked when she was built in the early 1930s.

would just have to wait for the rest, after all it was the depression. Charlie used the rest of his money to buy a new motor, a three-cylinder stationary Lister diesel which he had to convert for the launch. The engine was underpowered for a vessel of that size, but so was every motor in those days.

At 15.5 metres long the new launch was a big boat for those times and Claude didn't have a large enough shed so Charlie employed a couple of men and put up a shed especially for the job. This also saved him some money. The hull was built of inch-and-a-quarter [31 mm] treated white pine (kahikatea) planking, which is beautiful timber to work and was cheap and plentiful in those days. Old Charlie even had a piece of it soaked in water for six months to test if it was going to be all right.

Eighty years old, the *Noeline* is still going strong today, having outlived Charlie and most of his children – a tribute to Claude Wells's boatbuilding skills. Reportedly she was last sold for $50,000 – a long way from her construction cost of £300 in 1935.

Claude laid the keel and frames and did all the planking, decking and fastening, while Charlie was able to fit the boat out himself. However, towards the end he ran out of money while there were still some crucial bits to complete, including the fuel tanks. His temporary solution was to mount a 90-litre hot-water cylinder down below for a fuel tank, which held enough for a few hours' running at a time. Then he kept a drum on deck and would pump fuel from it periodically into the old water cylinder. It wasn't ideal and nearly caused a disaster once, as we shall see later, but at least it got him started. Instead of a piped water system he used earthenware jars and did all washing in a big basin. He even fitted a sail on the mast and used it a lot to save fuel (although he always said it was a hell of a thing to get up and down).

The new launch was finished at the end of 1935. The *Noeline* was a splendid boat and it is a testament to the skills of those who built her that she is still afloat 80 years later. There were two bunks in the bow then the engine room with the wheelhouse above, and a cabin aft for passengers and freight. He even had a toilet on board (not usual on launches at that time, but essential when carrying passengers). He could fit oil drums all along the deck and past the wheelhouse on either side as this was the only way fuel was carted around the area at the time. The deck area was large because with the mail and freight run he never knew what he would be carting from one day to the next.

Charlie always referred to his pride and joy as his "little canoe", which I think was an ironic reference to the big ships he worked on in the past. But the *Noeline* was more than just Charlie's new boat: it was a great new asset to the whole Sounds community. At last they had a reliable service, and they supported him well, so with mail, freight and fishing he started making money at last. Trampers wishing to have a look at one of the country's more inaccessible islands used to arrange to get Charlie to pick them up. A party of 25 from the Tararua Tramping Club chartered the *Noeline* soon after it was launched, in December 1935, to collect them from the steamer *Arahura* at French Pass then drop them at Cherry Bay, where they set up a base camp. Later he took them on a two-day cruise around the area before returning them to the steamer.

Young Charlie helped his father run the *Noeline* but Old Charlie also needed another boy and somehow he got a young lad called Bill Coulter from an orphanage in Nelson, promising that the boy would have better life and schooling with his family. The orphanage must have been glad to have one less mouth to feed but poor young Bill just went from the frying pan into the fire. He got no schooling and no pay, only food and hard work. Charlie didn't treat him much better than a dog.

Dave McLaren (left) and my mother Noeline with a friend who I only know by his nickname, Red. Here the *Noeline* is tied up in Nelson at a spot known as the Frog Pond.

Having a larger boat meant Charlie went to Picton more often and got back into his old ways, spending too much time in the hotel misbehaving. But he was getting older and losing more fights than he won, as the drink clouded his judgment. One time he was thrown out of the Federal Hotel late at night for being drunk and a nuisance to everybody. Angrily he went down the foreshore, grabbed a big lump of wood and threw it through the hotel window. He then ran down, jumped on his launch and headed home to French Pass. The next time he was in town, walking past the hotel with young Charlie, he looked in the hotel and smiled, hoping they had forgotten the whole incident or maybe had not been sure it was he who'd broke the window. But the publican spotted him and sent O.J. McManaway out of the pub to give Charlie a haymaker that knocked him out on the spot. O.J. was an old fisherman with whom Charlie had many a go over the years. Young Charlie must have got a fright seeing his father lying on the footpath, but he was to see a lot more of this.

Molly had been working on the *Peerless* since she was about eight years old, and later she and her sisters Noeline and Phyllis all worked with Charlie on the mail run too. As we will see later, the three girls acquired a certain fame in maritime circles. Although generally women were regarded as bad luck on a boat, the Jacobsen girls became respected as excellent seafarers in their own right. In time they even learned to run the launch service on their own when their father was sick or on one of his benders.

But the girls were still quite young when World War 2 broke out in 1939. There was a radio in the house by that

My mother Noeline with a boatload of blue cod.

Jean and Phyllis after a good day's groper fishing.

time and Charlie was glued to it whenever he was home, ranting and raving about how the war was going, I think he wanted to be back in the glory of it all, not saddled down with a bunch of kids, paying off a boat and stuck in the middle of nowhere.

Instead the war effort came to him and he found an important role right where he was. The government kept a system of coastwatchers – people located on remote headlands and islands around the country to watch the sea, operate radar stations and listen to the radio for signs of enemy shipping. Early in the war a German ship had laid mines around New Zealand and there had been several sinkings including the steamer *Niagara* off Auckland with more than £2 million worth of gold on board. Then there were the commerce raiders, German gunboats disguised as neutral shipping, that sank a number of New Zealand cargo vessels in the south Pacific, including the passenger liner *Rangitane* and the freighter *Turakina*, with the loss of many lives. Later an even worse menace loomed as the nation prepared itself for invasion by the Japanese.

So the government needed men on the islands around Cook Strait, and it needed someone to keep them supplied with provisions and equipment. Throughout this time Charlie worked his launch day and night as necessary to do his part for the war effort. The *Noeline* also delivered materials for the construction of gun emplacements throughout the outer Sounds, indeed Charlie did any kind of work for the war effort that he was asked to do.

MV *Noeline* hits the ebbing tide going into French Pass.

This also meant that the *Noeline's* underpowered diesel engine now became a problem, because the launch was part of the nation's defense network but not quite up to the job. The tide between the mainland and D'Urville Island flowed so fast the vessel couldn't make headway against it. This sometimes meant hours of waiting for the tide to change, or steaming all the way around the island, but the navy and army needed Charlie to provide reliable transport anywhere

The French Pass area, with some of the major places indicated that feature in this book. D'Urville Island is the landmass to the north and the mainland of the South Island is below. The Jacobsen family lived for many years at Camp Bay and Catherine Cove, and also at the French Pass township. Cable Bay is where my parents Jim and Noeline lived when they were first married.

MV *Noeline* at French Pass Wharf. Old Charlie to the left and Young Charlie as a boy to the right.

at any time. Government restrictions made it virtually impossible to obtain a better engine, especially during the war. However, even a government has sense sometimes, and in early 1944 someone in the Ministry of Supply found him a Gardner 4L2 diesel engine of 40 rated horsepower, which cost £1150, a great deal of money in those days. It took six months to arrive and wasn't designed for a boat but Charlie had adapted engines like this many times before, and did it again. Now the *Noeline* could go through French Pass at any time. Starting the new engine was tricky though. Charlie had to go down the engine room to hand-crank it, and it took two of his children to do it working together.

The daily routine was straightforward but time-consuming. They had to load and unload the steamers going through the pass, usually at 10 o'clock at night or three o'clock in the morning. The steamer would slow down and they would pull alongside to transfer cargo and mail up and down in a sling. There was a bit of an art to getting the boat alongside and some of the steamer captains weren't very cooperative and wouldn't slow down enough, making the job more difficult in darkness and bad weather. Then the *Noeline* would set off on a big circuit around D'Urville Island, Admiralty Bay and outer Pelorus Sound to deliver and collect the mail. They also steamed out to Stephens Island to supply the lighthouse keepers, about which more later. Livestock and dogs – they transported everything. Charlie delivered every Friday without fail for 25 years in a boat that really was too small for the job (certainly by today's standards) and in all weather.

Charlie announces his arrival with his bullhorn.

They had to let the people in houses and farms know they were coming, but the horn on the launch wasn't loud enough. So Charlie got a bullhorn and used to blow this as he approached. It was a distinctive sound and everybody knew it so they all came down to meet the launch, usually bringing hot scones, a billy of tea and making plenty of conversation because they were pretty lonely. Soon Charlie would have to cut them short as he had a schedule to keep. He and his crew never got hungry on the run as they were always offered more than they could eat and drink.

One day in July 1943 Charlie made an important zoological discovery. He saw a long, thin fish swimming close to the shore and was able to catch it by hand. The fish had extraordinary long fins, especially a dorsal fin like a crest: "I thought at first it had swallowed a piece of long kelp. Then it seemed to be able to draw it in (the dorsal crest) and throw it out again, so I knew it was not a piece of kelp. The colours were purple and black and it seemed to be twisted." He'd never seen anything like it before, and nor had the experts at the Dominion Museum to whom he

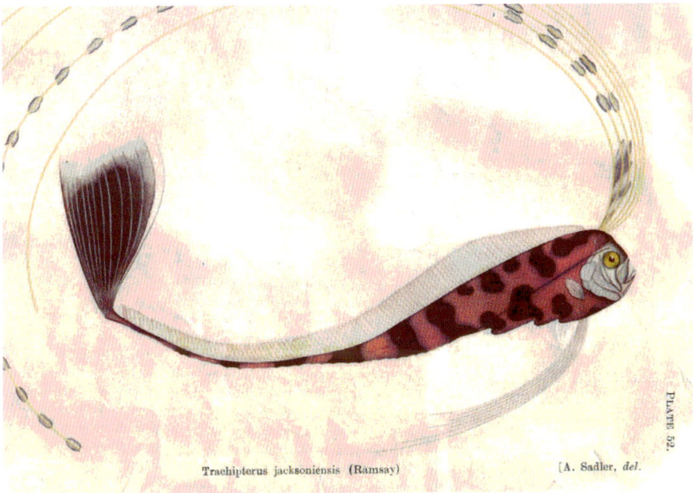

The fish Charlie discovered.

sent the specimen. It turned out to be a juvenile ribbonfish, *Trachipterus jacksoniensis*. Dr Phillips of the museum wrote a paper about it, and a museum artist painted a water colour of it.

One thing Charlie and Mary were really good at was making babies. By the time David was born in 1942 there were eight children and Mary was 41. Owing to her high blood pressure the doctor reckoned it would be life-threating for her to have any more. He pointed out that with Charlie 13 years older than her, at 54 years of age, he might not see the last of his children grow up and be able to support Mary if he died early in life. The doctor's solution was to talk Mary into having a hysterectomy. Many years later my father, who was a great storyteller and leg-puller, used to joke that "they had to sew old Mary up to stop Charlie filling her up with more kids". At the time we kids were too young to understand and I wondered how my poor old Grandma managed to pee.

The Jacobsen family's luck turned sour one day in 1941 when a landslide destroyed their house, though fortunately no one was killed or injured. They had some advance warning because it had been raining and blowing for days and Charlie knew this was mudslide or slips weather. He'd seen it happen many time before in rain-soaked ground under the weight of the shallow-rooted pine trees. Suddenly the loose ground and trees would begin to slide over the greasy surface of the rock underneath.

Showing the destruction of the Jacobsen house after the landslide.

The Jacobsen house after the landslide.

Charlie and Noeline walked up the valley behind the house to check the hillside. The house was close to the beach in the bottom of the valley where it narrowed. He thought there was some ground movement but wasn't sure if it was an ominous sign or not. Father and daughter sat there for a couple of hours in the rain under a bit of cover, just checking it was all right. Suddenly the hillside began to move and trees started toppling. Charlie quickly assessed the situation and figured the landslide would come down the back of the house. He knew Noeline could run to the house faster than him and sent her on ahead. She ran in the back door to where Mary was mixing up a batch of scones while the little ones were standing on chairs watching. Noeline yelled that there was a mudslide coming and that Dad had said to get all the clothes and bedding out of the house and along the beach, away from the line of the valley. Charlie soon arrived to find Mary busy emptying drawers and weeping as she always did at the drop of a hat. He phoned the neighbours for help and then chopped the phone off the wall, giving it to one of the children to take up the beach. They got most of their household belongings out, but then they heard a deafening roar as the slip gathered momentum. More mud and trees came with it as it made its way to the bottom of the valley where their house was right in the centre of its path. All they could do was watch as the slip picked up their house like a toy and destroyed it in a few seconds.

But at least Charlie had saved his family, like the hero he had been so many times in his life. Charlie and Mary now moved into the shed along the beach, keeping the youngest children at home while the rest went to live with other families around the area for a while.

So there he was with a launch, no house, and a bunch of kids. I bet he thought of getting in his launch and just leaving the lot behind as he had done in Greymouth. They had no money because it was all tied up in the new launch and they were still paying that off. In fact they didn't even own the land, because in those days Sounds people used to let friends who needed a place to live just build on their farms without title or even building permits. I suppose that arrangement was good for both parties: free use of the land in return for keeping an eye on that part of the farm. Now there was no way Charlie would get a bank to lend him money to build a new house. The last place to ask for money in those days was the bank, especially if you lived in such a remote place as French Pass on a block of land with no title.

Charlie built the family's new home on higher ground away from the landslide hazard. Or rather, his older children did most of the building work after he became injured while moving the timber to the site. The timber came from old army huts at the Cobb Dam construction site.

Soon the war was over and the army was disbanding. Everything was for sale to pay back the war bonds the government had put out to finance the war effort. There were plenty of old army huts coming up for sale by tender

as the army and navy had them built all around the country and they were no longer needed. Charlie heard of a batch of them at the Cobb Dam so he tendered £300 for four of them. He won the tender but was suddenly faced with a dilemma: how was he going to pay?

That's when a well-known and wealthy Nelson family came to the rescue. The Dimocks, who holidayed at French Pass every year, were great friends of Charlie's and when they heard of his plight they gave him an interest-free loan of £300 to pay back just whenever he could. Charlie concluded the deal, took the launch up to Takaka, the closest port to the Cobb Dam. With help of a couple of friends and his older children, he hired a truck, dismantled the huts and brought them down to the boat. Soon he had a whole lot of building materials ready at Fennel Bay, including some bits and pieces salvaged from the old house during the couple of weeks before the sea took it all away.

But while moving the huts, Charlie dislocated his shoulder. He had one arm in a sling and only the older children to help as they moved the materials to a new house site on more stable ground where no future landslide was likely to strike. Following Charlie's instructions they built the family's new home, humble though it was, with

The *Noeline* going through French Pass in the late 1940s with her new wheelhouse.

newspaper on the walls, only some carpet on the floors, and sacks cut open to cover the sarking. Later he built a tramway to cart things up and down. And so life continued for the Jacobsen family in their remote corner of the Sounds.

He put a new wheelhouse on the *Noeline* in 1947. Don Terry and my father Jim did the job, and I don't expect they ever got paid for it. Old Charlie was pretty good at getting the better of his relatives.

He was always a bit of a Jeckyll and Hyde character when it came to the booze. He didn't drink at home but when he hit town he used to go on a binge, especially when they went to Nelson in the launch for stores and equipment.

Once they were in town for a couple of days – Charlie, Young Charlie, Noeline and Phyllis. Mary didn't come. She avoided the sea like the plague: she never overcame the fear of small boats, plus I think the embarrassment over her husband's drunken behaviour was probably a factor too. By the third day the young ones were all waiting around for their elusive father, whom they hadn't seen since they arrived. They never knew where he'd been or with whom he had been socialising. But eventually, late in the afternoon, Old Charlie came staggering along the wharf, which made his family happy because now they'd be able to go home.

Young Charlie said, "I'll start the motor and get ready to go," but Old Charlie still had other plans. He said, " I have to go back to do some more business." He was at the top of the ladder down to the forepeak, the part of the boat where they slept and where he kept a stash of money hidden. He had only come down there to collect some more cash. Young Charlie knew this would mean another drunken night of fighting or womanising (or both), another lost day of fishing and more of the family's scarce cash wasted. In a sudden fit of rage he picked up a big spanner and hit his father over his head. Old Charlie fell flat down below. The girls scrambled down to tend to him and found that he was unconscious but not bleeding. Young Charlie told them to let the ropes go, started the motor and they were off on their way to French Pass.

The girls were pretty upset, wondering if their father would be okay and whether Young Charlie would get in a fight with him as soon as he came to. Young Charlie

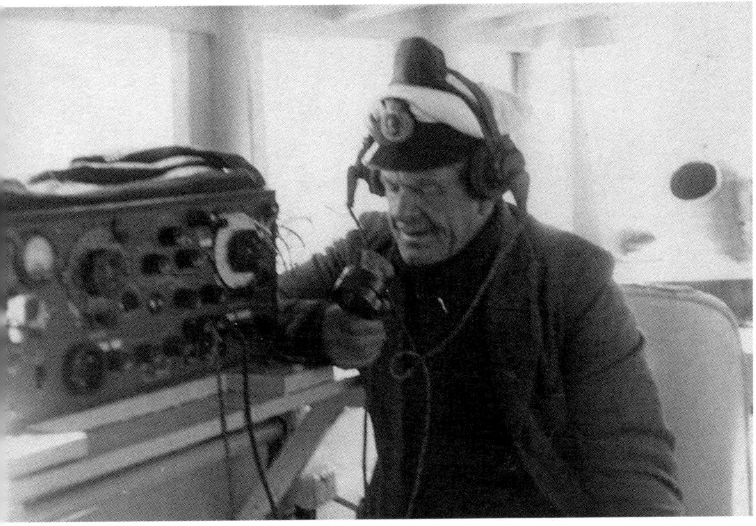

Charlie gets his first two-way radio for MV *Noeline*.

didn't say another word. He was a man now and ready for anything his father could dish up (in fact a few months after this incident he moved out of the family home for good).

Four hours later Old Charlie popped up out from below, rubbing the back of his head and asked where they were. The girls answered together, nervously, "We're just about home." Old Charlie responded, "Good; we'll be in time for tea." Obviously he had forgotten the whole incident. Young Charlie just smiled at that.

Noeline, Young Charlie and Phyllis.

The army huts weren't the only war surplus goods Charlie had a use for. He got a pair of two-way radios, one for the house and one for the boat. This made it easier to keep in touch and took away most of the feeling of isolation at sea, but was a double-edged sword. It also meant Mary could keep tabs better on her wayward husband and find out where he was making his money and then make sure the family got a bigger share of it.

Marine radio licenses were tightly regulated in those days and the rules and etiquette were strict. However, during the first week Charlie had the radio on the boat he was talking to anyone and everyone within range, like a kid with a new toy showing it off. This led to him getting a telling off from the maritime radio service, Wellington Radio. I think he was kind of hurt at being treated like a naughty boy.

Stephens Island, off the northern tip of D'Urville Island,

Lighthouse keeper and family going ashore at Stevens Island with a dinghy from the *Noeline*.

Looking down from Stevens Island at MV *Noeline*.

was a particularly important stop on the *Noeline's* circuit. It had been the location of one of New Zealand's most important lighthouses since 1894, guarding the western approaches to Cook Strait and the eastern approaches to Tasman Bay (and was one of the nation's last light stations to be automated, in 1989). During the war years the place was busier than ever with coastwatching and other secret activities. A naval radar station was built and staffed by more than 30 men who lived in a converted schoolhouse known as "the Palace". There was no secret about the lightstation on the island but the new buildings were all carefully positioned so they could not be seen from ships far out at sea.

During Charlie's time the light was operated by three keepers, some of whom had families living there as well. So a number of people were totally dependent on the service Charlie provided, and it was a responsibility he took very seriously.

Access to the island was never easy, with treacherous weather and no wharf or safe anchorage. The only way ashore was in a basket hanging on the end of a crane, or, in calm weather, by jumping on to the rocks. Usually passengers and goods were winched ashore, then there was a long walk up a hill 180 metres high to the lightstation and the keepers' houses. The place was infamous for high winds, and there are all sorts of stories about animals and objects being literally blown away.

My Auntie Jean told me a story about a particularly scary time they had landing stores at Stephens Island on a rough day. It's a hell of a place when there's a big sea running, and Charlie couldn't raise the lighthouse keeper – no matter how hard he blew on his bullhorn, the wind just seemed to tear the sound away. If he didn't deliver his cargo he would have many hours of steaming there and back next day to fulfil his duty. So he decided to put Jean ashore to alert the lighthouse keepers. Of course, since there was no one to operate the crane, Jean, who was then a nimble girl of 14, had to jump ashore. She waited on the bow of the boat as it heaved up and down with the waves, then jumped, landing in seaweed on a rocky ledge.

By the time she had got the lighthouse keepers down to work the crane the weather had become even worse and unloading was a very difficult job, but they finished the task and now only had to get Jean back on board. Noeline at the wheel brought the boat as close in as she dared, with Charlie on the bow trying to grab Jean as she leaned outwards. But soon even the daredevil Charlie had to admit the sea had won the day, and Jean was marooned until the weather improved. As they steamed away they watched her and the lighthouse keeper make their way in the wind and rain up the steep track to the warmth of the keeper's house with his wife and family. Jean was stuck there for a whole week and not picked up until the next weekly mail run.

The crane on Stevens Island.

But that's not quite the end of the story. Poor old Mary got a hell of a scare when Charlie and Noeline got home that night. I have already mentioned she was a big sook, and she was already in a hell of a state when the boat appeared, late, in the bay. They had no radio to keep in touch in those days. Then, after they put the launch on the mooring, they climbed in the dinghy to come ashore and Mary looking from the top of the hill could see one of the girls was missing! By the time they had rowed ashore, pulled the dinghy up the beach and started up the trail to the house Mary was in a hysterical state, crying and screaming and shaking. It was always her worse nightmare that one of her children might be lost at sea, and it took some time to make her understand that her Jean was alive, safe and sound but marooned on Stevens Island.

Auntie Jean had another story, about the time when Charlie's temper nearly was the death of them all. I mentioned earlier how the launch just had a small fuel tank down below, which they had to fill every couple of hours from a drum on deck. Charlie always intended to replace it with a bigger fuel tank, but took his time about it. They had an alarm clock to remind them when it was time for a top-up. On this occasion they were in heavy weather and when the clock went off Charlie tried to bully my mother into letting him take the wheel so he could send her out on deck in the wet and cold to do the pumping. But she was not a little girl any more. She had grown into a young woman who knew her own mind and would no longer always let her father tell her what to do without question. So Charlie put on his sou'wester, swearing and cursing about what "useless bitches" his daughters had turned out to be, and went out on deck. He unscrewed the top of the drum and dropped the hand pump in, working the handle back and forth, but nothing happened. The old pump had given up the ghost owing to lack of maintenance. For a moment Charlie stood, trembling with rage and frustration, with his back to the weather and one of his Capstan Cork cigarettes hanging wet out of his lips. Then he pulled the pump out and raised it above his head to throw over the side … but just in time he caught Noeline's eye through the wheelhouse window. She fixed him with a steely gaze and just shook her head slowly. For a moment it was touch and go as they all knew it was the only pump on the boat and they'd be lost for sure if they didn't get some fuel down below fairly soon.

Phyllis, Kathleen and Noeline.

Soon Charlie came to his senses and was pulling the pump apart on the wheelhouse floor. Noeline slowed the launch right down so her father had a more stable area to work without the boat pitching, and so the tank in the boat wouldn't suddenly run out of fuel as the small amount remaining in the tank slopped about. If this happens on a boat you have to bleed the injectors to get the air out of the fuel line and that would have set Charlie off again in a tantrum. Eventually he got the pump repaired, they filled the fuel tank and were able to continue their journey safely.

As the children grew up and started leaving home I think Mary got tired of being stuck in such a remote place without any company, so she wanted a change of lifestyle. The opportunity came up to lease a guest house at French Pass and she jumped at it. As well as more company it meant better housing and even a school next door for the younger children. The boarding house wasn't very busy but it did give her some income of her own. It was a pleasant lifestyle and they even had pet tuataras living under the floor (just imagine the Department of Conservation letting them get away with that today!) It was also easier for Charlie to run his launch business from there as it was the main wharf of the area.

Pet tuataras that lived under the boarding house at French Pass.

Old Charlie kept on defying the Grim Reaper. He even survived a nasty incident when the *Noeline* caught fire at the wharf. One of the locals came running into the house to raise the alarm and the whole family ran to their stricken launch to see smoke pouring out of the aft cabin entrance. Of course, the launch was the only asset Mary and Charlie had, and it was uninsured so if it was destroyed they would be ruined. There was no water supply connected to the wharf and the only fire extinguisher was in the cabin that was on fire. The kids got there first, wondering what to do, then Charlie came running, pushing them all aside and jumped on board and disappeared into the smoke-filled cabin. At this the kids starting crying, thinking their father was going to be burnt to death, but then they heard the fire extinguisher go off and the smoke from the cabin eased. Then Charlie staggered out, his face burnt and most of his hair gone, and collapsed on the deck. A couple of men carried him back to the boarding house and called the district nurse. Apart from the burns on his face he was all right after a couple of days in bed.

Young Charlie with his wife Kathleen (*née* Aston).

Phyllis, Noeline and Kathleen.

Eventually father and son fell out over the way Old Charlie treated his daughters and Young Charlie found himself banished from the house. The only way he could see his mother was to visit when he knew his father was not there. With no money and only schooling to the age of eight years, he boarded at French Pass and started fishing from a borrowed dinghy. Soon had enough money to buy his first boat, the *Mizpah*. He married an older woman, Kathleen Aston, a member of the family he was boarding with. She was a strictly religious Catholic and very much a mother figure to him. The two of them owned fishing boats and became very well off, but never had any children. Kathleen helped out the family a lot and looked after her nieces and nephews throughout her life. Young Charlie too was a good man and loved very much by his brothers and sisters. When

Young Charlie's *Mizpah* coming in to French Pass Wharf.

Young Charlie's first boat, the *Mizpah*.

he died in 1992 he left everything to his family including his nephews and nieces. His estate was worth about $500,000, a lot of money in those times. I have fond memories of the man that treated us like the children he never had.

As his daughters grew up Charlie gradually came to rely more on them to run the boat. Molly became the first woman in New Zealand to get an AB's ticket and Noeline the first with a skipper's ticket. Both girls ran the launch service all on their own at times. Later, in 1947 Phyllis earned the respect and gratitude of the Anchor Shipping Company after taking part in a rescue at sea when the ship *Taupata* was nearly wrecked near French Pass. Captain Williams of the *Taupata* expressed his utmost appreciation and the company gave her an engraved wristlet watch – a handsome gift in those days when timepieces were expensive and not something most young people owned. There was even an article about them in the national weekly magazine *Free Lance*, headed "Girl Mariners of French Pass: Remarkable Feats of the Jacobsen Family". "Hard work does not bother them and the way they get it done would put many a man to shame."

Phyllis, Noeline and Jean.

David McLaren, a family friend who was a regular visitor to French Pass in his childhood recalled another incident when he and his mother were on the *Noeline* going to meet the steamer:

> The tide was running southwest at full strength, the sky was pitch black and we were tucked up behind the light on the end of the pass reef. Then suddenly we were sucked on to the concrete base of the light. Somehow we had missed the light

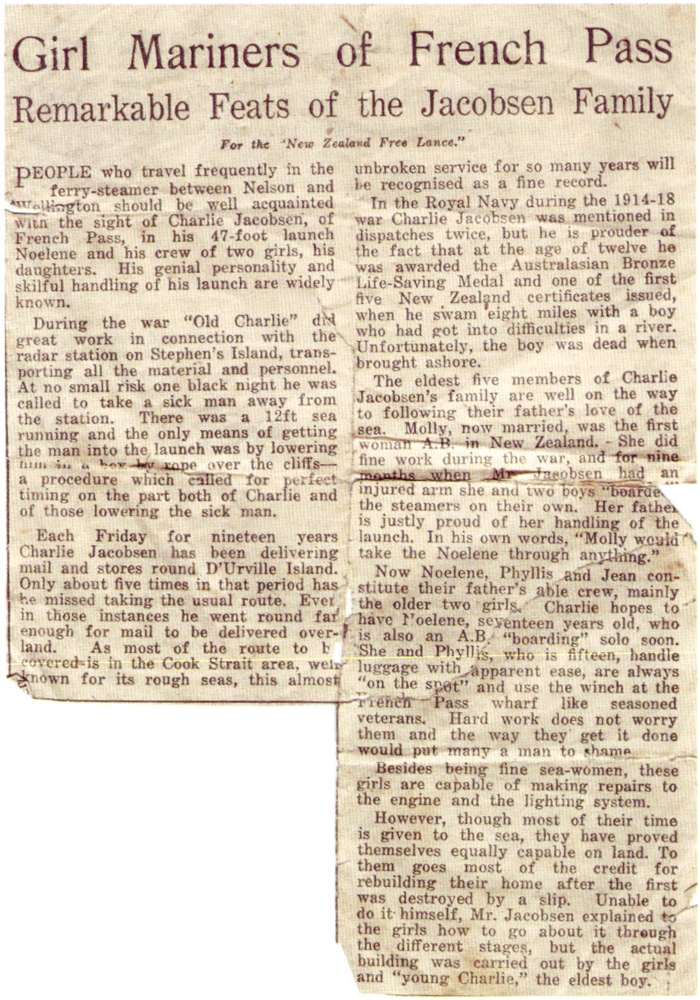

Girl Mariners of French Pass

Remarkable Feats of the Jacobsen Family

For the "New Zealand Free Lance."

PEOPLE who travel frequently in the ferry-steamer between Nelson and Wellington should be well acquainted with the sight of Charlie Jacobsen, of French Pass, in his 47-foot launch Noelene and his crew of two girls, his daughters. His genial personality and skilful handling of his launch are widely known.

During the war "Old Charlie" did great work in connection with the radar station on Stephen's Island, transporting all the material and personnel. At no small risk one black night he was called to take a sick man away from the station. There was a 12ft sea running and the only means of getting the man into the launch was by lowering him in a box by rope over the cliffs—a procedure which called for perfect timing on the part both of Charlie and of those lowering the sick man.

Each Friday for nineteen years Charlie Jacobsen has been delivering mail and stores round D'Urville Island. Only about five times in that period has he missed taking the usual route. Even in those instances he went round far enough for mail to be delivered overland. As most of the route to be covered is in the Cook Strait area, well known for its rough seas, this almost unbroken service for so many years will be recognised as a fine record.

In the Royal Navy during the 1914-18 war Charlie Jacobsen was mentioned in dispatches twice, but he is prouder of the fact that at the age of twelve he was awarded the Australasian Bronze Life-Saving Medal and one of the first five New Zealand certificates issued, when he swam eight miles with a boy who had got into difficulties in a river. Unfortunately, the boy was dead when brought ashore.

The eldest five members of Charlie Jacobsen's family are well on the way to following their father's love of the sea. Molly, now married, was the first woman A.B. in New Zealand. She did fine work during the war, and for nine months when Mr Jacobsen had an injured arm she and two boys "boarded" the steamers on their own. Her father is justly proud of her handling of the launch. In his own words, "Molly would take the Noelene through anything."

Now Noelene, Phyllis and Jean constitute their father's able crew, mainly the older two girls. Charlie hopes to have Noelene, seventeen years old, who is also an A.B. "boarding" solo soon. She and Phyllis, who is fifteen, handle luggage with apparent ease, are always "on the spot" and use the winch at the French Pass wharf like seasoned veterans. Hard work does not worry them and the way they get it done would put many a man to shame.

Besides being fine sea-women, these girls are capable of making repairs to the engine and the lighting system.

However, though most of their time is given to the sea, they have proved themselves equally capable on land. To them goes most of the credit for rebuilding their home after the first was destroyed by a slip. Unable to do it himself, Mr. Jacobsen explained to the girls how to go about it through the different stages, but the actual building was carried out by the girls and "young Charlie," the eldest boy.

Phyllis, Noeline and Jean and the newspaper cutting about them.

and nosed out into the full force of the incoming tide, at the wrong angle. The *Noeline* lay over on her port side and it was a miracle that no one was lost overboard.

The Friday mail run around the island was always different, and often a rough trip. On these runs the crew lived on tea with lots of sticky condensed milk, which always seemed to be served at the roughest point in the trip. Then there were the "doorstop" white bread sandwiches with quince jam. I couldn't look at quince jam for years afterwards. I loved condensed milk and black tea individually but in the rough seas, with the smell of diesel plus Charlie pissing in the bilge, it was even a bit much for me.

As a result of these forays to French Pass I took a youthful shine to Phyllis and ended up staying a lot at the Jacobsen homestead. The Jacobsens took me in as one of their own for a short part of my life and the experience has stayed with me. I used to go out with Young Charlie fishing on his boat the *Mizpah* around the back of the island, hauling up the cod three at a time with hand lines. I can still remember the blisters.

Coming back one night, when we arrived at the mooring the other kids were in the dinghy yelling that Charlie had sunk the *Noeline* off Pepin Island, near Nelson. Young Charlie and I took off to the rescue. Old Charlie had been fishing for snapper off Kahurangi Point with Bill Coulter as crew. They had come back to Nelson and unloaded, retired to the Customhouse Hotel for a session and then decided to head back to French Pass. They left in daylight and a Tahuna resident up on the hill saw the *Noeline* go out through the Cut [the harbour entrance] and do a lazy circle, then straighten to carry on northeast along the Boulder Bank towards home. Charlie had obviously gone to sleep momentarily but woken up again quickly. However, he soon dozed off again, by which time he was near Pepin Island and the *Noeline* ran straight into a rocky bluff. Bill Coulter was asleep in the forepeak when she hit and reckoned by the time he got his feet on the floor the water was already up to his knees. Charlie managed to back the boat off the rocks and found a beach where he was able to drive her ashore. It was high tide and they jumped off the bow as she settled.

Young Charlie and I arrived in the early hours of the morning, by which time the tide had gone out and an army of helpers were on the job. Someone had made a wooden box pump and there was a continuous bucket brigade emptying out the boat. By the time the tide came in again there was a canvas bandage around the sprung planks on the bow and a boat either side with rope slings under the *Noeline*, while the *Mizpah* was in front with a tow rope. The procession arrived back in Nelson later in the morning and the *Noeline* was patched up once more (this was the fourth time she'd been aground). The old valve radio, which was high in the wheelhouse, was about the only useful thing to escape the dunking.

My father Jim Horncastle and old Charlie Jacobsen inspecting damage to MV *Noeline*.

In another incident Charlie went to try and salvage a barge drifting in Cook Strait after its tow rope broke in heavy weather. He took Noeline and Phyllis to help, but by the time they found the barge the weather had taken a turn for the worse, and just getting on board it in the heavy roll was dangerous. Not realising the barge was empty, Charlie accidentally allowed himself to get into the trough of a wave while the barge was on the top. It came down the wave faster than he expected and crashed into the launch, smashing a lot of the planks along one side. The *Noeline* made a desperate

MV *Noeline* loses a man overboard.

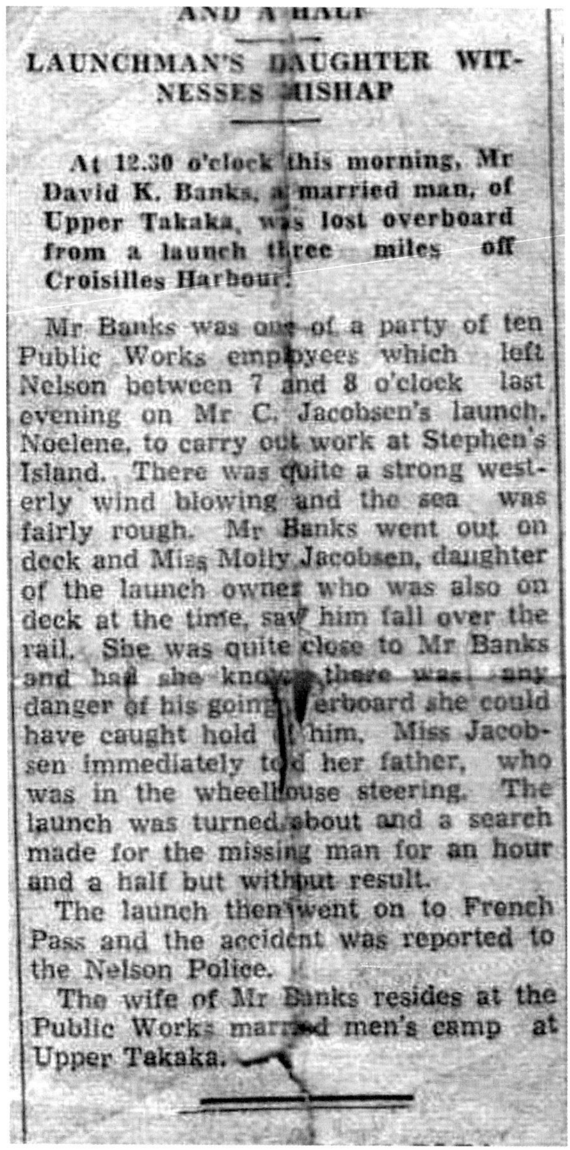

AND A HALF

LAUNCHMAN'S DAUGHTER WITNESSES MISHAP

At 12.30 o'clock this morning, Mr David K. Banks, a married man, of Upper Takaka, was lost overboard from a launch three miles off Croisilles Harbour.

Mr Banks was one of a party of ten Public Works employees which left Nelson between 7 and 8 o'clock last evening on Mr C. Jacobsen's launch, Noelene, to carry out work at Stephen's Island. There was quite a strong westerly wind blowing and the sea was fairly rough. Mr Banks went out on deck and Miss Molly Jacobsen, daughter of the launch owner who was also on deck at the time, saw him fall over the rail. She was quite close to Mr Banks and had she known there was any danger of his going overboard she could have caught hold of him. Miss Jacobsen immediately told her father, who was in the wheelhouse steering. The launch was turned about and a search made for the missing man for an hour and a half but without result.

The launch then went on to French Pass and the accident was reported to the Nelson Police.

The wife of Mr Banks resides at the Public Works married men's camp at Upper Takaka.

run into a sheltered bay where he made a temporary repair job using bits of canvas and wood. After that he was still keen for another try at getting the barge, but his daughters had had enough and talked him out of it.

Incidentally, after this incident Charlie took the boat to the boatbuilder Jack Guard for repairs, and that's how my parents first met, as my father was working for Jack at the time. I might never have come into being had it not been for that botched salvage attempt.

Another time Molly was at the wheel of the *Noeline* when something made of iron, like a knife or something, had been left too close to the compass, causing her to get a wrong reading, and she ran on to the rocks near Cape Soucis, near Croiselles Harbour. Charlie managed to pump the boat out, drove her ashore and they ran canvas under the bow, tacked it on and drove her back to Nelson.

In September 1944 they lost a man overboard while taking a party of workmen from Nelson. Charlie, Noeline and Molly were bringing the men to French Pass and kept them down in the cabin because most of them were drunk, but the only one who was sober went up on to the deck and somehow fell overboard. They circled round for two hours and the girls were in a hell of a state about it.

Charlie was never one to miss out on any handy resources, including flotsam and jetsam. Even a dead whale washed up on a beach was grist to his mill. He cut up the blubber and boiled the oil out of it in a fire under an oil drum, no doubt a smelly job but the oil he got was good for cleaning boots and other things. He also salvaged the teeth, and made a chess board and a walking cane and clothes hanger out of the jawbone.

CHAPTER 13

Leaving French Pass

Mary and Charlie Jacobsen in the 1950s after moving from French Pass to Picton.

The tombstone of the twin sisters I never had: Phyllis and Carol, who were born prematurely on D'Urville Island, died shortly after birth.

Charlie and Mary kept the house at Fennel Bay, along with the mooring for their launch, when they moved to French Pass. They now had the lease on the boarding house. Charlie was getting older and the older girls Molly and Noeline had married and left home. At 65 years old he was starting to slow up and it was hard to get anybody to work like his daughters, just for their keep and no pay.

By 1948 Mary had had enough of the primitive living and isolation of French Pass, and her parents had passed away, leaving her the family house in Picton. My guess is that her parents knew this was the only way that they could give their daughter a better way of life. She told Charlie he could come too if he wanted but made it clear she was off and taking the family with her whether he liked it or not. Jim and Noeline decided to move too, as this was just after the tragedy of losing their first two daughters who were born premature and died at birth, and they didn't want to live in the isolation of D'Urville Island any more.

Charlie was getting on in years so he had had very little choice. They relinquished the mail contract and made the move to Picton. However, Mary couldn't shift into her new home straight away as her brother Eric was living there and she didn't have the heart to throw him out as he was still shell-shocked from World War 2. So for the meantime she bought the lease on a run-down rat-infested old flop house, the Newton Guest House. It was a real dive, with a few war veterans living there long-term while it also provided a cheap bed for anyone requiring short-term accommodation. Picton was a busy port in those days as hardly anyone travelled by air between the North and South Islands; but with Charlie and his mates loafing around and drinking all hours of the day and night the Newton can hardly have been anyone's preferred place to stay.

The move wasn't as simple as you might think. It wasn't just a matter of listing their houses on the market with a real estate agent and expecting to find a buyer with ready money. Neither Charlie and Mary nor Jim and Noeline actually owned the land on which their houses were built. It was owned by some farmer. In Charlie and Mary's case at least, the house had probably been built only with the permission of an earlier farmer, who was now long dead. The next generation of ownership would be a son or grandson who probably didn't want them there anyway, especially since these beautiful bays were now beginning to be worth real money. So the Jacobsens and Horncastles not only moved themselves: they pulled down and removed the family house as well, intending to rebuild in Picton. You can

The Jacobsen family in the 1950s. From left to right: Mrs Zilla Bary, Mrs Myrtle Freeth, Eric Jacobsen, Mrs Molly Dann, Charles Jacobsen ("Old Charlie"), David Jacobsen, Mrs Mary Jacobsen, Charles Jacobsen ("Young Charlie"), Mrs Noeline Horncastle (the author Graeme Horncastle's mother), Mrs Phyllis Ivamy and Mrs Jean Rutherford. The only surviving family members today 2015 are Jean, Myrtle and David.

Charlie and Mary's house in York St, Picton, as it appears today. It's now in much better condition than in the 1950s but still holds happy memories of the times I stayed there as a child.

imagine the work, pulling down two houses and sheds full of fishing gear and engine parts, and taking boatload after boatload to Picton. The *Noeline* had a limited cargo capacity but Jim and Charlie worked away at it. Charlie managed to recover enough materials to build another house and bought a section at Waikawa, just east of Picton, and set Jim (my father) a hard-working builder and carpenter, to work for him. Unsurprisingly, Jim never got paid for all his work. Charlie had never paid his daughters to work on his boat and didn't see why his son-in-law should be any different. So Charlie got himself a house to rent out and kept Jim at arm's length with a promise to "fix you up sometime". He didn't even offer his son-in-law the use of the house he'd built for nothing. I think that was pretty miserable of him, especially when his own daughter had just suffered the loss of two babies.

Then Jim and Noeline moved to Blenheim (perhaps Charlie's meanness drove them out of Picton at last), and their story is told in my book *Horncastle's Suitcase*. Charlie

Charlie, Young Charlie, Jim Horncastle, Eric and David.

and Mary were quite well set up in Picton, but Charlie was restless and at a bit of a loose end, no longer having the mail run or the endless odd jobs that needed to be done when they had lived at French Pass. He was desperate for a bit more adventure before he became too much older. For a while he kept himself occupied getting the *Noeline* ready to sell and doing a bit of charter work. He got some satisfaction and income out of running fishing trips and sightseeing for the tourist trade. He also got a mail run around Queen Charlotte Sound for a while but it didn't work out.

Old Charlie and his eldest daughter Molly.

I mentioned earlier how Charlie once found a stranded whale and got oil and whalebone from it. After moving to Picton he was in close contact with the New Zealand whaling trade as this was centred nearby. He was finding it hard to get work for the *Noeline* and the locals certainly didn't need more competition from yet another boat. However, it seems nobody wanted the work that was available carting whale meat.

At the eastern end of Tory Channel on Arapawa Island was a bay called Te Awaiti. Joe Perano had set up a whaling station there in 1911 and it was run after his death by his sons Gilbert and Joseph, closing in 1964 when there were too few whales left to keep the business going. The whale blubber was boiled up for the oil but there was no use for the meat.

However, there were large farms in Port Gore, a bay between Tory Channel and Blenheim with no road access, and the farmers realised they could get the whale meat cheap for dog tucker, so Charlie got the job of carting it. His son Eric was on the *Noeline* on their first trip into Te Awaiti and said the smell made him feel sick. The whalers used to leave the meat on the end of the wharf for them, already cut in cubes about half a metre a side. It was messy to load and then they had to steam around, anchor the *Noeline* then load the meat into the dinghy and row it ashore. Here the farmers had cutting tables under the trees and the whale meat was cut in strips then hung in the trees to dry.

Then a new money-making opportunity came up with the 1951 waterfront dispute – the biggest event of its kind in the history of the nation. The lockout dragged on for five months, with coastal freight paralysed throughout New Zealand. The watersiders were out of work and other workers walked off the job in support. Even the inter-island ferries were tied up as the crew joined their fellow workers in a show of solidarity. The Prime Minister, Sid Holland, used the army and navy to keep essential services running, but there was still a desperate shortage of freight carrying capacity across Cook Strait. Like many other launch owners in the region, Charlie seized the opportunity to start running freight. Trade unionists call this "scab labour" but I don't think Charlie gave a damn what they thought. Being the veteran of World War 1 and a conservative sort of a bloke, he probably had no sympathy for the watersiders, who he reckoned had an easy life and deserved everything that was now happening to them.

So he started running freight between Picton and Paremata, a small fishing port near Wellington. It's actually a shorter run between Picton and Paremata than between Picton and Wellington, but Paremata is too shallow for big ships. It also had the advantage that there was usually no freight being handled there, so they could come and go without attracting much attention. For crew he had his son Eric and his "slave," Bill Coulter. This worked well and they made many trips. At first they only took light loads, playing it safe as the *Noeline* was not designed for carrying freight in open waters. She had little storage space below decks anyway so most cargo had to go on deck, which limited what they could carry.

But as the dispute dragged on, the demand for carrying freight became higher and he took more risks, overloading the small launch to make more money. Soon he had not just one accident, but two – and the second one very nearly cost him and his crew their lives.

The first was when going in to Paremata one night he hit a bridge pile and sprung all the planks in the bow. It was just about low tide at the time, so he ran the *Noeline* up the beach and sent Eric to get the local boatbuilder, Alf Sanders, who lived close by. They got him out of bed in the middle of the night, he recaulked the launch and they were able to refloat her on the next incoming tide. But it was a close shave and they had got off pretty lightly this time.

For their next trip they filled the vessel with dry goods like food items, then loaded up the decks with metal pipe, toilet bowls and other cargo that could stand getting wet. It was the biggest load he had ever carried and way too top-heavy. Charlie headed for the nearest pub to have a few drinks before sailing, leaving Eric and Bill on guard. "If any bastard gives you any trouble just show him this," he said, handing them a length of iron pipe each. They weren't happy at all about waiting – they just wanted to get out while the going was good. But old Charlie quite enjoyed having the odd confrontation with a few angry workers who knew about the "blackleg" freight services. He could usually stand up for himself and after a few drinks he would be spoiling for a fight.

But while Charlie was getting himself a skinful, a large crowd of locked-out workers arrived at the pub. There were far more of them than he was used to dealing with at once. Even when he was full of booze Charlie could size up the odds pretty quickly and knew discretion was the better part of valour, so he made a run for the wharf, where Eric and Bill were waiting, ready and eager to cast off. Feelings were running very high by now and men were desperate to see the dispute end so they could get back to work and provide food for their families. More and more of them gathered on the way, egged on by one of the union leaders, and there were no police anywhere to control the angry crowd. But Charlie hadn't run out of tricks yet and was quite prepared to take the law into his own hands. He was wearing the World War 1 Luger pistol that he'd taken off a dead German, in a holster inside his jacket. It was loaded and ready to fire. He told Bill to get the .303 rifle out of the cabin and load it too. Now the scene was set for a real confrontation.

The union man, who was doing all the talking and rabble-rousing, said they were coming aboard to throw the freight over the side and smash up the launch. Charlie told Bill to point the rifle at him and told him to "shoot the bastard if he puts a toe on board my bloody boat". Then, pulling out the Luger, he jumped on top of the wheelhouse and yelled at the crowd for silence.

Everybody went very quiet at once when they saw the guns. Charlie said something like this: "I respect your right to strike, but I have to make a living too. I may look an old man to you but I assure you we will shoot you if you come on board. I killed a lot of Germans in the war while defending our country so you all could enjoy the way of life you have in New Zealand today. I don't want to kill anyone today but I will if I have to, so back off!"

The crowd looked first into the face of the old man and then at Bill, who they realised would do exactly as he was told, such was his loyalty. None of them wanted to stop the first bullet. They knew they were beaten and slowly backed off and were soon gone. Fortunately this incident blew over without any repercussions. It didn't even make the newspapers and the police certainly didn't want to charge a war hero.

Charlie still had a load of freight to get across Cook Strait, and as they cast off they were heading into worsening weather. It's only a short hop from Paremata to the shelter of Cape Koamaru, about 40 km as the petrel flies, but it's right across the throat of Cook Strait, one of the most dangerous stretches of water in the world if you get the weather wrong. The other launch owners thought better of it and decided to stay in port and take the risk that the angry mob might return. But not Charlie, who loved to skite that his boat could go anywhere in any sea. He drove his small launch straight into a screaming southerly and within an hour realised he had made one of the biggest mistakes of his life. Wave after wave smashed into the windows of the wheelhouse and it could only be a matter of time before a window would be stove in and then it would all be over. Even trying to turn around and head back was dangerous because the launch was so top-heavy it was liable to capsize. So for the second time that day his actions had put him in danger, this time including his son and a crewman as well. The three of them now found it necessary to stay on deck, steering from the outside position. They closed the wheelhouse door and jammed it shut for fear of taking water down below.

The only chance was to try to time the waves and turn the *Noeline* around while in the bottom of a trough between one big wave and the next. At that moment she would be in relatively calm water and the wind would drop slightly, but he would have to time it just right and there would be no second chance. Picking his moment, he swung the wheel hard round but the launch could only do 6 knots and was slow to respond. They all saw it coming: a giant wave rearing up out of a green wind-whipped sea. Before they had time to even react the wave threw the launch over on its side and it rolled upside down while the deck cargo came loose and lurched to one side. Charlie found himself under water, but clear of the boat, and swam to the surface. There were no lifejackets but Charlie found Eric and swam with him to a floating hatch. Meanwhile the *Noeline* had lost all her deck cargo, which was just as well because otherwise she would never have come back right-side up, and they could only see her now and then as waves and spray hid her from view low down in the water. Fortunately the motor was still running, with the wheel still hard round as it had been when he was turning the boat, so the launch was going in circles around them. Looking around for Bill, they could see his head above the water and registered the peculiar fact that he seemed to be moving behind the boat, at the same speed. Then they realised he had his leg tangled in the ropes, which turned out to be a stroke of luck. Being a fit, wiry young man Bill was able to turn himself around slowly and pull him himself back towards the moving vessel. Once he was on board he took the wheel and soon picked up Charlie and Eric.

But even then they were still far from safe, as the *Noeline* was wallowing dangerously in the heavy sea. As soon as Charlie jumped on board he could tell from the feel of the boat that she could turn over again any moment. To their horror they realised the wheelhouse was full up with water from the bilges, even above the level of the windows. The hatch down to the engine room had popped open and let the bilge water out while the boat was upside down, then when it came upright the hatch abruptly snapped shut again under the weight of all that water. This made the boat once again just as top-heavy as before. The pressure of all that water kept the sliding door shut so they couldn't even open it to let the water out.

But here Charlie's long experience served him well, because instantly he knew just what to do, and he didn't hesitate, even though it was a drastic action and made a terrible mess of his precious boat. He grabbed the fire axe, which was still secured on the wheelhouse wall, and smashed every window so the water could pour out. Then he took the axe to the sliding door, smashing it too so the rest of the water could drain away. Now that the boat wasn't so top-heavy, he was able to turn it back toward the North Island so they had the wind and sea behind them.

He told Eric to take the wheel. They weren't out of trouble yet. The *Noeline* was surfing down the huge waves and Eric had to stop the boat from sliding on to its side (broaching). Charlie and Bill went down into the engine room, where they could just see the motor above the water that was still sloshing about in the compartment. Charlie knew he had to keep the engine running or they'd lose control. The fuel supply was watertight and bulletproof but the air intake wasn't. He took it off and put on a piece of pipe to keep the air intake well above the water level no matter how much the boat rolled. Then he looked at the pumps, which were working but not fast enough. With the engine running flat out, the flywheel was picking up water and throwing it up against the underside of the deck. If only there was a hole for it to be thrown through. Desperate situations require drastic measures, so he grabbed the axe again and started chopping a hole in the deck. Eric and Bill thought the old bugger had finally gone mad – they were too young and inexperienced to realise what he was doing. But old Charlie had turned a few corners in his life and they soon figured out that there was method to his madness. The flywheel acted just like a pump, throwing water on deck and over the side of the boat.

Soon they had the situation more or less under control, though it had been a very near thing and it was only after eight hours that they were safely making their way up the Porirua Harbour towards Paremata, where they grabbed the first mooring. Literally just as they slipped the mooring rope around the bollard the Gardner engine came to a grinding stop, completely seized – talk about lucky; or unlucky perhaps, because that was like the last straw.

After that Bill and Eric got jobs on fishing boats while Charlie fixed the boat. At least for a while they wouldn't have to work with a man who put their lives in jeopardy. Charlie put the *Noeline* on the slip, where he spent the next three months fixing it and rebuilding the engine. By the time he had finished the lockout was over and New Zealand was returning back to normal. There never seems to be any winner from industrial action and in Charlie's case all the money he'd made was spent on repairs.

There is an amusing sequel to this story. Many years later I had a pub in Picton, Oxley's Tavern, which I leased from one of New Zealand's two big breweries, DB. The rival beer company was Lion, and one time their brewery workers all went out on strike. Soon there was no Lion beer available anywhere in New Zealand (but the government of the day did not regard this as a big enough crisis to call in the army to keep the breweries going). Anyway, the strike created a real problem for a local pub owner whose supply contract only allowed him to sell Lion beer. He asked me to help him out on the sly, and I pumped some of my beer into a mini-tanker early one morning so he could keep his bar going and not go broke. The word got out (I think some of his customers must have been able to taste the difference – I certainly could!) and an old guy, Ted Stammers, came and abused the hell out of me: "You're a scab, just like your grandfather was back in 1951!" What long memories some people have; I think he'd been nursing that petty grudge for 20 years. Anyway, I read the riot act to this guy. I told him he could go and drink somewhere else if he still had an issue over something about my dead grandfather. But he didn't change watering holes – he continued to prop up the bar at Oxley's just the same as he had done ever since he was old enough to drink.

I was born a few months after the 1951 waterfront strike ended, though this was certainly not a big event in Charlie's life. By that time he was too old to go back fishing and the family had had a gutsful of helping him on a promise to pay

Mary and Charlie on a well-earned holiday.

MV *Noeline* as a tourist boat in Picton.

when the good times came along. Most of his family were now in Picton. Living in town meant they could have real jobs and get paid at the end of the week so they were no longer under his thumb. Times had changed and the coming generation was getting more confident. The girls were married or had boyfriends; Mary had the boarding house; Charlie had lost the power to play tyrant and family bully any more.

He tried to sell the *Noeline* but there wasn't much demand for boats at that time. It wasn't suitable for a pleasure launch, and you couldn't get a commercial fishing license at that time (the government kept the fishing industry very small, with no new licenses until 1963). Charlie was worn out, too old to change, and had no money to embark upon new ventures. He was a lost soul, yearning for his previous life as a war hero and master of his small ship that serviced the French Pass area where he had been held in such high regard. He was spending too much time in the pub telling his stories to the the younger generation, who were sick of this old has-been arguing about anything and everything.

Before long he even started coming home covered in blood, the loser instead of the winner when he got into a fight.

Men got away with much more rude treatment of women in those days and I'm not going to repeat some of the ways my grandfather referred to women. One of his more mild jokes was: "When a man's got a gutsful of beer from a day of drinking, all women look good and I think that was why beer was invented."

He leased the *Noeline* out to local fishermen but it never worked out and most of the time he got nothing for it. Mary too was having a hard time, without enough paying guests and with too many people sponging off her. Between her large family, her brothers and their families, and Charlie always having a couple of mates down in their luck, she never really stood a chance. She was too much the mother figure and never tough enough to turn anyone down. But she did have the moral courage to finally boot her brother Eric out so she could at least move into her own house. After all that hard work there she was back sleeping in the old bedroom she had left all those years before. Now she became resentful towards Old Charlie: he had filled her up with kids every year and led her a life of heartache and overwork with very little to show for it.

All in all Old Charlie's shares were pretty low with family and the world in general, but still he was far from finished. He faced up to some hard facts like the need to make some big changes and compromises. First he really had to sell the *Noeline*, even if that meant dropping his asking price. As a result he got less than it was worth. It was also a lot less than he had wanted. But £1,800 was still a lot of money then, more than two years' pay for most men, and he no longer had the costs and worries of running the boat. But even that didn't work out later as the buyer, from a local fishing company, only paid Charlie a £500 deposit when he took the boat and he never got the rest. I don't think the buyer was a bad man; it was just one of those deals that went wrong.

Then a new obsession came to him, out of left field, one that would occupy him for the rest of his life. He got the uranium bug.

CHAPTER 14

The great uranium adventure

It all goes back to when Charlie was a boy and his father did quite a lot of gold digging and was interested in minerals. That's how he started to learn something about mining. Wandering around on D'Urville Island in 1924 Charlie had noticed what was known as the "mineral belt", a zone of different rock running 37 km from one end of the island to the other. It was greenish and flaky and the soil formed from it was very poor. Trees didn't grow well in it and in fact you could recognise the mineral belt anywhere because the vegetation growing in it was stunted, like on land suffering from bush sickness. The mineral belt was part of a rock formation that also runs through the mountains near Nelson and then joins the greenstone (nephrite) zone of the west coast. These kinds of rocks (called ultramafics) could include valuable minerals, and sure enough, after a bit of searching Charlie found some outcrops of serpentine and asbestos on the island. He carted boatloads of talc from Catherine Cove to the Tarakohe limeworks for experimental crushing but nothing came of this. Asbestos was used to make building board (fibrolite) and serpentine is used in fertilisers, so he thought it might be worth his while to stake a claim.

He took some samples and went over to Wellington by the steamer from French Pass, to seek advice from the Department of Mines experts. On the way he met someone who told him Fred Cassin was the man to talk to, and arranged an introduction. It turned out that Cassin was a very experienced prospector and miner who would be a very useful contact in later years when the uranium rush was on. Meanwhile, nothing more came of Charlie's serpentine or asbestos because there were other places in New Zealand where these minerals could be mined more cheaply.

Later, Charlie had some experience with gold (see Chapter 6) and he always dreamed of striking it big. But it was uranium that gave him his really big thrill in his old age. Quite a few prospectors and miners got the uranium bug around that time. It was all because of the Cold War. America and Britain were flat out building stockpiles of nuclear weapons, and for that they needed uranium. Lots of it.

Since the 1940s people had been prospecting for uranium all over the world. The uranium bug reached New Zealand from Australia, where serious prospecting had begun even before the end of World War 2. The British and Americans asked Australia to find as much as they could to help arm the west against the red peril. Looking back on how the Soviet Union has turned out, it all seems ridiculous now, but at the time communism really seemed a massive threat. The Russian premier Nikita Krushchev was pretty scary with the things he used to say about the western world – "we will bury you," and so on. We needed the bomb to keep that kind of menace at bay. In 1948 the Australian government even posted a reward of up to £25,000, a fortune at the time, for the first discovery. It worked, and by the mid-1950s mines were operating in the Northern Territory (Rum Jungle), Queensland (Mary Kathleen, the richest mine of all) and South Australia (Radium Hill). Around 1965 the US bomb production peaked, with an arsenal of more than 30,000 nuclear bombs. Uranium was also used to make plutonium, for even bigger and better nuclear bombs that could destroy the world not just once but many times over. Uranium also had a peaceful use in nuclear power plants and at that time people still believed nuclear power was going to be a wonderful safe cheap clean source of energy.

In the early 1950s uranium was the new gold, and Charlie knew enough about gold to feel confident about having a go at uranium. When he heard about the big discovery at Rum Jungle in 1949 by a man called Jack White, he dreamed about doing the same thing himself in New Zealand.

An article in *Time* magazine of 15 September 1952 summed up the excitement:

> From Darwin to Melbourne, the word had got around that Australia's vast, tropical Northern Territory was bursting with uranium. Hundreds of adventurous young men from Australia's overcrowded southern cities, plus many an old gold fossicker from West Australia, were making their way up through the desert by jeeps, horse-drawn wagons, on horseback, even in airplanes. In Darwin, Geiger counters were sold out as fast as they came into the store. One newspaper advertised counters: "Find Uranium and Make Your Fortune"...

To find uranium the first thing you need is a Geiger counter, an electronic instrument that detects the tiny amount of radiation coming out of uranium ore. It was originally invented by two men called Hans Geiger (hence the name) and Ernest Rutherford, New Zealand's famous Nobel Prize-winning scientist (who incidentally was born at Brightwater, near Nelson). A Geiger counter displays the amount of radiation on a dial or it makes clicking noises – the more clicks, the more radiation. You've probably seen them in scary films where a guy holds the counter up close to a container full of radioactive waste and the clicks get ominously louder and louder until they sound like hail falling on a tin roof. Anyway, Charlie got himself a Geiger counter and an old 1934 Chevy truck, and still had a couple of hundred pounds left over from the sale of the *Noeline* so he gave the last of it to Mary, and this got him back in her good books. I think he was really approaching all this like a man trying to make a new start all round. Then he looked up Fred Cassin again. And so begins the story of how two old men made their way into the history books as the first discoverers of uranium in New Zealand.

Charlie's Geiger counter, which is today among the memorabilia on display at the Pavilions Hotel.

Fred was in his 80s by this time but still as keen as mustard. He came over from Wellington in November 1955 and they met up for a trip to Charleston, near

The old European Hotel, where Charlie and Fred stayed on the night before their big uranium find in the Buller Gorge, 1955.

Westport. They wanted to start there because it was already known that the levels of radioactivity were slightly higher than normal – a likely sign of uranium but not proof of anything. I think Fred also wanted to find the site where he had worked in a gold mine many years earlier, but they were unable to find it as the west coast takes back its own back quickly: even man-made things can be gone in 20 or 30 years. Charleston had been one of the gold rush areas of the 1800s, with about 5,000 miners in its heyday, all gripped with gold fever. There had been lots of shops, pubs, bawdy houses and all the other things that make a frontier town but it was gone now, with only a few holiday shacks and one old pub left. The narrow two-storey old building looked ready to fall over, with no paint but a faded sign still visible reading “European Hotel”.

Fred and Charlie made this their base and spent long evenings there drinking and exchanging stories of boats sinking, war adventures and so on, probably not letting the truth get too much in the way of a good yarn. Each day they went out prospecting but had no luck. On their last day, a Sunday, they went back to the pub, had some lunch and packed up their gear ready to drive back to Picton via the Buller Gorge so Fred could catch the ferry back home.

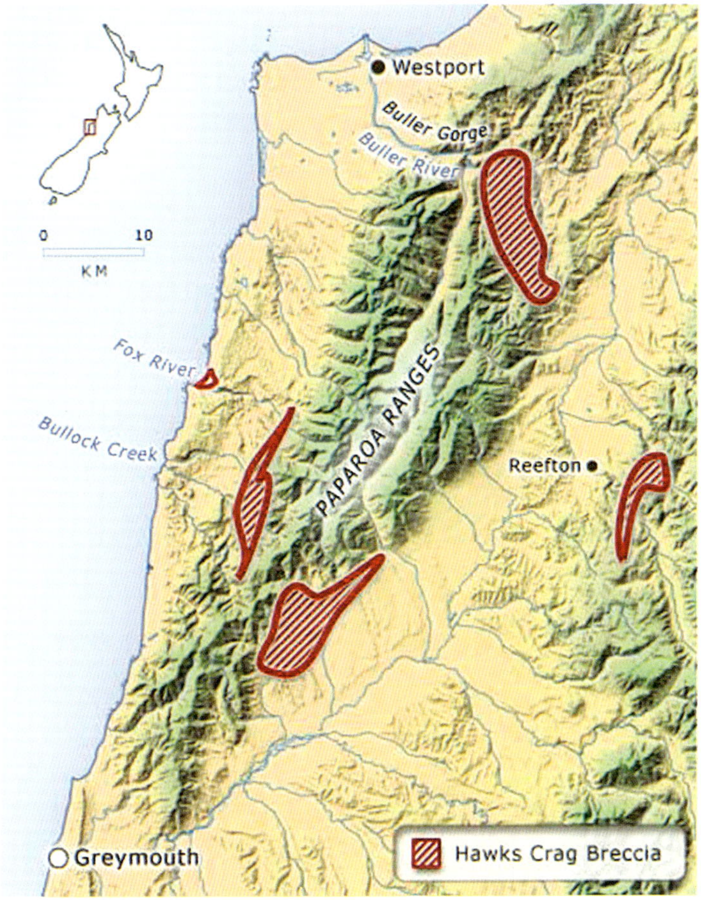

Map of the areas where most of the early uranium prospecting was focused. The red areas are exposures of the Hawks Crag breccia, a kind of volcanic rock that contains traces of radioactivity.

The Buller Gorge is a great drive, with a huge river flowing through steep forest-clad hills. There's a famous scenic spot called Hawks Crag where the road literally runs through a slot cut in the side of a cliff 15 metres above deep green swirling water. Charlie stopped for a leak near this spot, and just out of idle curiosity he put the Geiger counter on some rocks there, simply because they looked a bit different. The count (number of radiation clicks per second) was twice the normal or "background" rate, which was a significant increase, though nothing to get really excited about. But it was enough to make Charlie decide to spend a few minutes more exploring.

As he drove up the road, stopping five or six times, the radiation count increased all the time. In Charlie's own words:

I said to Fred that I had always thought that there had to be uranium somewhere in the district as the count was over three times the background rate but I never expected to find it so soon. I was driving the truck and doing about 30 miles [50 km] an hour when all of a sudden one of those coloured rocks flashed across my vision on the right-hand side of the road. It looked like a picture I had seen of uranium ore and was only 20 feet [6 metres] or so away. I stopped the truck and Fred asked what I was doing. I said that I had just seen something and was going back to have a look. He waited in the truck while I went back and put my counter on the face of rock ... you can just imagine the shock I got when the needle on the dial went hard over! I had only experienced that level of happiness once before but I will not describe that here. I took more readings and they were a bit patchy but some of them were very high. I took about six readings before I was satisfied that I had found uranium. [This locality was Batty Creek.]

It was no use calling out to Fred, as he was very deaf, so I went back to the truck. I tapped him on the shoulder and told him I had found something very good and he should come back and have a look. We walked back and put the counter on the face of the outcrop and he just gasped as the needle went off the dial. He told me I must have blown the valve and I replied that was what I had thought at first but when we backed off the reading fell, then we moved closer and it went up again, so we knew it was still working properly. Fred just watched the dial in amazement. We did that half a dozen more times before we were convinced we had located something worthwhile, and then we shook hands on the discovery.

I tried to knock a piece off with a cold chisel but could only get a few small chips. We went a short distance further up the road to the Berlins Hotel where we were able to borrow a pick and crowbar, then came back and managed to knock off several pieces. By this time it was too late to get Fred back to Picton in time for the ferry that day so we decided to stay the night at Berlins. We went back to the hotel and had a few beers, keeping very quiet about our find though inside we were bursting with excitement.

Next morning we got up early, about 4.30, because we did not want anybody to see us, got some more samples and went back at the hotel for breakfast. We then left for Picton, arrived about 12.30 pm.

We went to Wellington … I rang Parliament and asked for the Minister of Mines, Mr Sutherland. The young lady said he was away and that Mr Shand [was standing in for him]. As it happened I knew Tom Shand personally, he was a farmer from Kaikoura and MP for Marlborough, and when he asked me what I wanted I said I'd prefer not to talk about it over the phone so he told me to get a taxi and come up and see him right away.

I showed him several pieces of the ore that I had bought up with me and asked him to ring the DSIR and find out if anybody else had found any ore with a high enough count to be worth mining. They confirmed that my sample was the first, and Mr Shand gave me a signed document to that effect.

AUCKLAND, NEW ZEALAND, NOVEMBER 23, 1955

Uranium Prospector

Mr C. Jacobsen, who, with Mr F. Cassin, made the first discovery of uranium ore in the Buller Gorge, tests a boulder on the bank of the Buller River. Other pictures on the subject are on pages 23 and 30.

Charlie hits the news big time.

It was a moment of great triumph. Although Charlie's main object was to be the first to discover uranium in New Zealand, I doubt he thought that he would actually be the one to do it, or that it would be so easy.

Charlie continued his story: "A count over 1500 was an economic deposit. My samples read around 400 which was low, but it was early days yet and I was confident we would find richer deposits. It's always like that with gold: you start off finding small bits, and then find where it's more concentrated, and I was sure it'd be just the same with the uranium too."

The story was a news sensation throughout New Zealand, and even overseas too for a short time. There was a big article with their photos in the *Weekly News*,

From the *Free Lance* newspaper, November 1955. Charlie is holding the Geiger counter while Fred Cassin has the sample of radioactive rock in his hand and is listening to the clicks through an earphone.

Charlie and Fred study rock formation as crowds gather to look at the find.

which was like the equivalent of network TV news in those days. Geiger counter sales skyrocketed again. The town of Westport thought there was a boom going to happen and the local ice cream factory sold “Uranium Ice Cream”. One news reporter couldn’t resist dressing up the story a bit by implying they had been on a bender at Berlins and

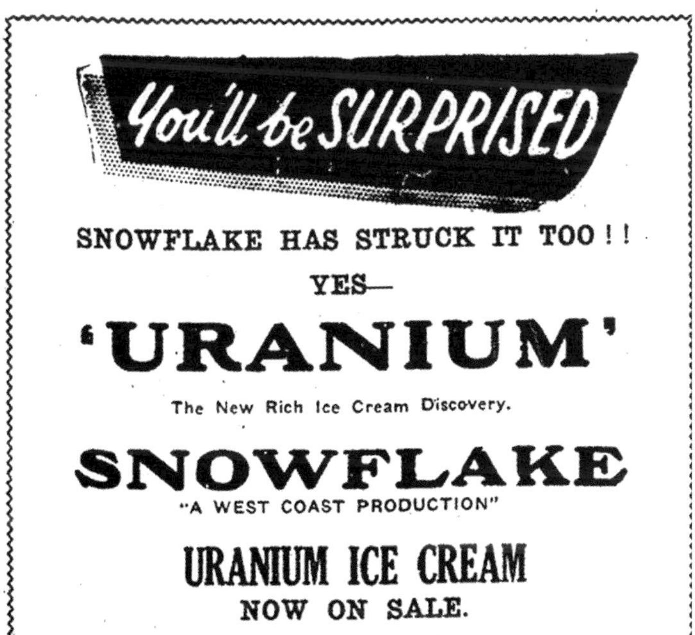

Everybody got on board the uranium find.

had fluked on the uranium when they stopped to relieve themselves on the side of the road. The kind of story that makes good folklore but in fact Berlins was further up the road from where the find was made.

All the attention and sudden fame went to Charlie's head. However, Fred was an old miner who'd seen it all before and told Charlie not to get too carried away. There was no guarantee that the uranium would turn out to be widespread or payable. The initial levels of radiation were quite low, so what they had found was a prospect, not a promise. It would cost money to stake the claim and have it surveyed and registered, and even if everything continued

Charlie enormously enjoyed all the attention including this newspaper photograph taken when he was invited to survey the area from the air, and was very proud of the letter he received from the Prime Minister, Sid Holland, acknowledging his find. (opposite).

well it could take years to prove the deposit, let alone to start mining it.

He said something like, "Look, Charlie, we're a couple of old chaps who've made the headlines by finding the first uranium in New Zealand. We've made our point.

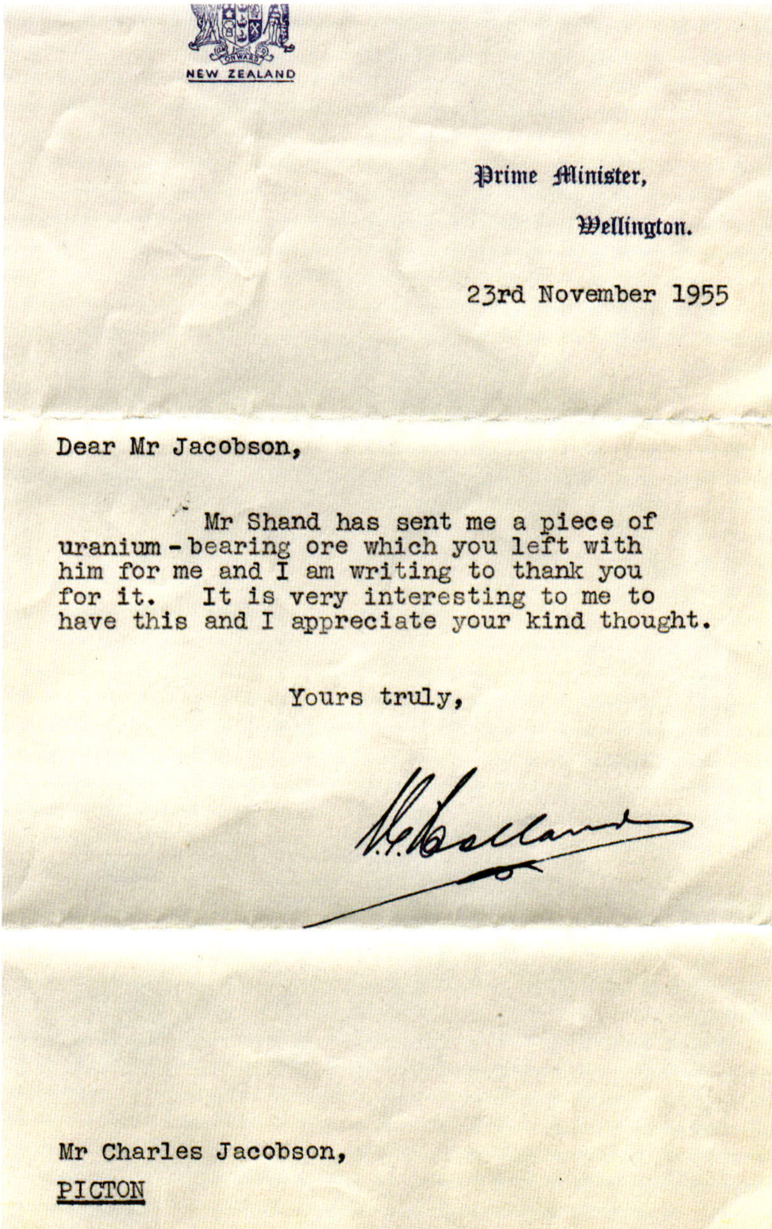
NEW ZEALAND

Prime Minister,

Wellington.

23rd November 1955

Dear Mr Jacobson,

Mr Shand has sent me a piece of uranium - bearing ore which you left with him for me and I am writing to thank you for it. It is very interesting to me to have this and I appreciate your kind thought.

Yours truly,

Mr Charles Jacobson,

PICTON

The government's going to give us something for the discovery. Let's just let it go at that."

However Charlie saw the whole thing differently. He thought he was on to a bigger thing than winning Tatts twice in a row. Just look at the photos of him taken around that time – a man suddenly full of vigour and looking ten years younger. He was even open and friendly to rivals: "While we pegged our claim off two young fellas pegged off 500 acres across the river from us. I met them in Westport one day and they showed me a piece of rock with a reasonable count. I told them to keep on looking around about where they found that because it's most likely they would find the outcrop there … "

Charlie and Fred stake their claim.

Further investigation of the find went on for years with extensive sampling of the radioactive rocks. Unfortunately the uranium content was too low for economic mining.

They staked their claim, and watched uranium fever build up throughout New Zealand. But soon the optimist Charlie and the realist Fred had a falling out. Charlie wrote down what happened, but unfortunately it is mostly incoherent, probably because he was so upset at the time. He was obviously lost – didn't know how to go about staking a claim, had to deal with lawyers, analysts and other experts who would blind him with science.

Soon after, in May 1956 prospectors employed by Buller Uranium, a subsidiary of Lime & Marble, reported three finds of radioactive boulders and outcrops in the lower Buller Gorge. A Westport company called Uranium Valley found traces of uranium at Fox River and in the Paparoa Ranges. Over the next four years the New Zealand government granted more than £35,000 to the search. Buller Uranium used their grants to cut tracks or for helicoptered supplies to four prospecting camps. Uranium Valley built two huts in the Paparoas, at Bullock Creek and Pororari.

A secret agreement between the Crown, the United Kingdom Atomic Energy Authority (UKAEA) and Buller Uranium was signed on 11 March 1959. The UKAEA was to investigate the Buller Gorge uranium deposits, and would have first right of refusal over any uranium found in New Zealand. In return for this, the Poms financed the venture

Mary with a piece of the "uranium ore", perhaps dreaming of the wealth to come.

plus they probably paid a bit more into the government's coffers. During 1959–60 they did some trial mining at a spot across the river and high up the hill from Charlie and Fred's find. They set up a camp with bunkhouse, drilling equipment and a rock crusher. Between September 1959 and March 1960 they drilled 10 short tunnels by jackhammer. Chemical analysis, however, revealed that concentrations of uranium oxide were too low to support underground mining operations. In August 1960, after spending £17,775 on uranium prospecting on the west coast, the UKAEA terminated their agreement.

In the end Charlie and Fred's great find was worthless. They had just fluked on a local warm spot for radiation. That radiation did not only come from uranium, but also from a patch of radioactive zircon, so a lot of those clicks on the meter weren't uranium at all. Still, my grandfather really was the *first* person to find uranium in New Zealand. Even if it was not rich enough to be worth mining.

There was still the matter of the government award, and the following year they were each given a paltry £100, which was another disappointment. In the end the government relented and gave them another £400 each but by that time old Fred had gone to that great gold mine in the sky so the money went to his estate. The total reward of £500 each was a significant amount, although nothing like the Australian award of £50,000 that Charlie thought was a sure thing. Kiwi uranium was not going to be made into bombs to incinerate millions of Reds after all, nor was it going to make the Jacobsen dynasty rich. Apart from a reasonable whack out of the government they got something in the landscape named after them – Mt Cassin and Mt Jacobsen.

Over the next decade, several companies undertook exploration programmes (some subsidised by the government), but the results were disappointing. The grade of mineral-bearing rocks was very low, and no new areas of radioactivity were found.

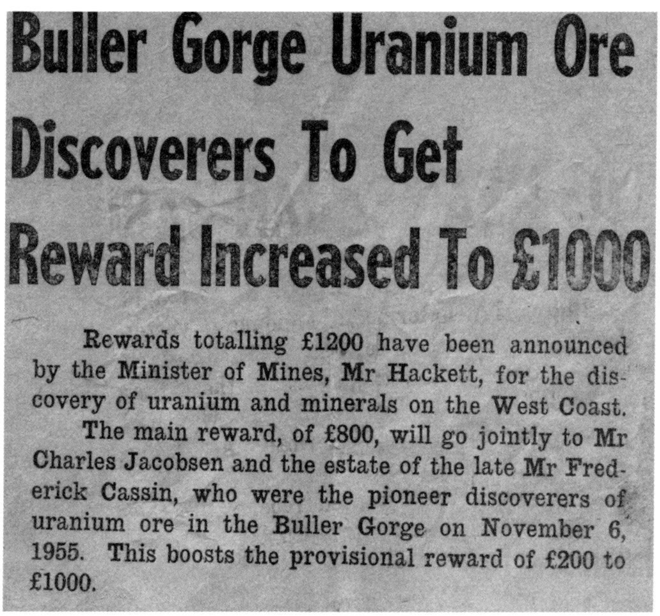

Buller Gorge Uranium Ore Discoverers To Get Reward Increased To £1000

Rewards totalling £1200 have been announced by the Minister of Mines, Mr Hackett, for the discovery of uranium and minerals on the West Coast.

The main reward, of £800, will go jointly to Mr Charles Jacobsen and the estate of the late Mr Frederick Cassin, who were the pioneer discoverers of uranium ore in the Buller Gorge on November 6, 1955. This boosts the provisional reward of £200 to £1000.

The government gave Charlie and Fred a paltry £100 each at first for the find, then later increased it by another £400 each. But it was nothing like the amount Chalie had hoped for and he was bitterly disappointed.

Charlie's dream turned out a disappointment and it took its toll on him. For years afterwards he carried a piece of rock in his pocket that gave a reading of 152 ticks a minute on the Geiger counter. In a shed at home he had over a ton of rocks taken from different places and enjoyed demonstrating their radioactivity to anyone who would listen to him on his old hobby-horse.

Deep down I think he knew he was too old ever to reap the reward of the thousands of pounds that he thought he would receive when the actual mining started, but for the first time in his life I think he was looking to a future beyond his own times. He was thinking of his children and the good life they could have with all that money and how they might forgive him for his harsh treatment of them when they were young.

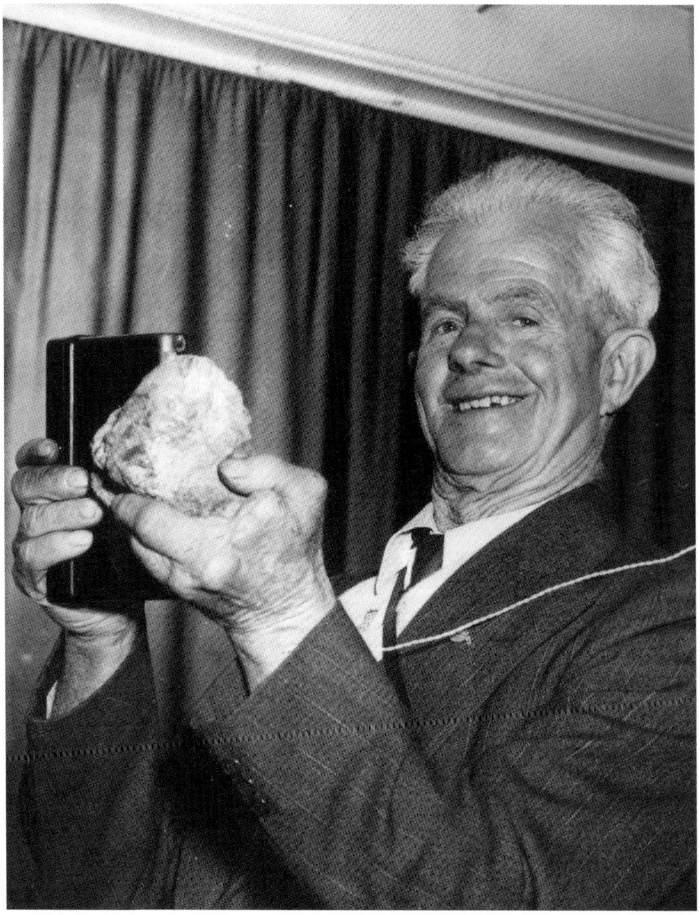

Charlie never tired of re-living the glory.

CHAPTER 15

Charlie's last days

During the last days of all the attention over his uranium find, hope faded and old age began to catch up with him.

Charlie spent his last years helping with various projects around Picton. He helped to rebuild the foreshore, operating the harbour dredge, built a merry-go-round out of an old truck diff and helped build a skating rink. It's all been changed again several times though and none of it is left.

By this time his vegetable garden was one of the few active interests he had left in life. Then one afternoon he had a heart attack while grinding up whalebone for fertiliser. The ambulance came and took him to hospital. Mary and the family visited him that night and promised to see him the next day. He asked for Phyllis last and told her where his memoirs were recorded in a notebook, and said to keep it until the right person came along to write a book out of it. That's where I came in, though it wasn't until 40 years later.

When they rang next morning they found out he had passed away in the night. The date was 24 March 1960. A man who had lived from the Boer War and two world wars cheating death so many times was dead at 73.

His story has been waiting for 55 years to be told.

Whenever I think about my grandfather Charlie I think what a miracle it is that I'm even here. Because he came that close to death so many times it's no exaggeration to say he had more lives than a cat. He nearly died of drowning about a dozen times while swimming or seafaring. Twice he

Even at an advanced age Charlie still was often bright-eyed and full of life.

narrowly missed being on major shipwrecks that involved great loss of life. During World War 1 he was torpedoed twice, wounded three times in battle and managed to survive four different theatres of war. In later years he nearly

Charlie and Mary at one of their daughters' weddings.

One of the last photos of Mary, taken some time after Charlie died in 1960.

Zilla, Noeline and Phyllis, 1970s.

wrecked his own launches and fishing boats so many times the actual number is lost in the mists of time. Charlie took part in dangerous activities like high diving and even had a near-death experience involving drugs long before he learned to poison himself slowly by drinking. Then there were the many people whose lives Charlie saved or nearly saved from drowning. He was successful every time except one, and that was the time he received a medal.

It would only have taken one of these events to turn out differently and my mother would never have existed and thus nor would I. This not only fills me with a sense of wonder but also makes me think how many other people never existed because of the war and other hazards that killed so many men of Charlie's generation. All the other relations everyone would have had, but who never existed because one of their parents was killed. It doesn't pay to think too long about things like that, it just makes my head spin.

It seems in those days there was more opportunity for adventure too, as you will have seen in these pages. Sailing, swimming, long-distance cycling, gold mining, discovering uranium and getting into all kinds of fun and mischief … Charlie may have been a bit of a bad old bastard, especially by today's standards and the way he treated his family, but he certainly had plenty of adventure and actively played a role as a second-generation New Zealander. Certainly he did his bit for the country – doing his patriotic duty, helping develop a young nation and helping people in remote places keep in contact with the world. His story is interesting and I think I would still find it interesting even if he hadn't been my grandfather. Charlie's name also lives on through the Jacobsen Cup, a trophy he donated in the 1950s to the NZ Amateur Roller Skating Association after he was involved in building a skating rink on the Picton foreshore. In the late 1990s the trophy was transferred to SkateNZ and is now awarded annually to the club that wins the most points in artistic events.

The cup Charlie won all those years ago, with all its history, still in use today as a trophy in Lower Hutt roller skating.

Well this was the man; his blood is mine and I see some of the things I have done in life run parallel to his. In our extended family of his descendants you see him everywhere. So was he a hell raiser or a hero? Surely you would have to agree with me that he was both. When the descendants meet it is not long before the subject of "Old Charlie" comes up somewhere and I believe this is the stuff folk stories are made of. So Charlie, rest easy now. Your story is told, late but never too late for the history books of time.

This cottage on Collingwood St, Nelson, was built by the first Jacobsens around 1857. Its current owners, Bruce and Pam Thomas, have been restoring it since they bought it in 1975. This photo was taken at the Jacobsen family reunion in 2009.

Right: Graeme Horncastle, the author, standing at the front gate.

The author at Uranium Point in the Buller Gorge with a restored 1937 Chevy truck just the same as the one Charlie had in 1954.

Left: David Jacobsen (Old Charlie's youngest son) with the Geiger counter and some rock from the Buller Gorge find of 1955.

Below: A family gathering at my parents' farm in Karamea, about 1956. Standing: my uncle Les; my father. Seated, from left: Les, Tom, Mum holding Mary; my cousin Barry, Old Charlie; and myself, holding the cat.

INDEX